Teach Your Children Well
A Parent's Guide to Encouraging Character and Integrity

Madelyn Swift

Also by Madelyn Swift

Discipline for Life: Getting it Right with Children

Getting it Right with Teens

Teach Your Children Well
A Parent's Guide to Encouraging Character and Integrity

Madelyn Swift and Victoria Mathies

childright

Childright
Southlake, Texas

An Essentials Series Book

Childright
2140 East Southlake Boulevard, PMB 640
Southlake, Texas 76092

Printed in the United States of America
First printing: September, 2001
Second printing: January, 2004

Library of Congress Control Number:
2001135445

Swift, Madelyn
Teach Your Children Well: A Parent's Guide to Encouraging
Character and Integrity
ISBN: 1-887069-08-9

The paper used in this publication meets the minimum
requirements of American National Standard for Information
Sciences - Permanence of Paper for Printed Library Materials,
ANZI Z39.48-1984

Childright website address: www.childright.com

To Tim, for questioning the subtleties of character and for showing me courage and love as action; to Kris, for making me realize the importance of character and for teaching me about loyalty and unconditional love; and for my husband John, for so consistently demonstrating integrity and generosity and for always being there for us.

To Sheila, for teaching me that being a mother was the most important job of my life; to Rachel, for reminding me over and over again of the uniqueness of each human being; to Philip, for showing me in the past year what acceptance and courage look like; and to my husband David, for being there throughout it all.

And to men, women and children of integrity and good character everywhere.

Acknowledgments

My first thanks go to Julie O'Keefe who is friend, editor and associate. Her help in both my professional and personal lives is the single greatest factor that allows me to write. To Bob, Shannon and Nicholas, who share her with me, I also owe thanks. As well, I appreciate Tammy Stripling who helps make the office run.

Our gratitude goes to all of the authors whose works are cited; they were helpful to us in ordering and clarifying our thoughts. Special thanks to Jean Clarke who so generously shared her work. We also wish to thank the parents who continue to share their concerns, thoughts, and insights with us.

To our families, the Swifts, John, Kris and Tim and the Mathies, David, Sheila, Rachel and Philip, we owe our greatest debt. To our husbands, John, who made sure I was geographically close to Vicky, and to David, who keeps us healthy and in good wine, we owe much. To the five children who inadvertently sent us on this journey, we are most grateful.

"Teach your children well." —Crosby, Stills, Nash & Young. Giving Room Music, 1970.

Foreword

Over the many years that Madelyn and I have been friends, we have discussed together a revolving door of issues, conflicts which seem continually to confront us as parents. Some concerns have come and gone, and returned to visit us again and again. We have had, however, one consistent theme to our conversations: have we helped each of our children to develop the skills and character they need? What should our role be? How can we know *when* to act and *how* to act when we see that character is at issue? How will we know if we've contributed positively to their character development? Of course, there are no hard and fast answers to these questions. We have come to a belief, however, that in our daily interactions with our children, we have been influencing and affecting the development of their character, sometimes positively, sometimes negatively.

Our children would tell you that over numerous pots of tea, in both sunny and cloudy weather, we have also shared with each other the stories of our lives: stories about our children's moments of grace and moments of failure; stories about our children's friends, whom we love and care about; stories about ourselves and our siblings as children; stories from the community which have touched both of us; and stories which have helped us to clarify what it means to be a good person.

This book will reflect the flavor of these discussions. Sometimes as parents we want a pep rally, someone to tell us sharply, yet compassionately, to shape up and get motivated. Sometimes we have a specific problem and we talk about it with everybody while we gather information and feedback, and finally set upon a course of action. And, sometimes we need to hear other people's stories, stories which give us imaginative opportunities to see our worst fears acted out and our most deeply desired wishes fulfilled. Reading or hearing a story can help us to fill in the blanks around the advice we've received and the learning we need to do.

Most of us rear our children on stories. We do this, not just because we seek our children's literacy but because we know the soothing qualities of a good story. Who hasn't chosen a story book (Maurice Sendak's *Where the Wild Things Are*, Judith Viorst's *Alexander and the Terrible, Horrible, No Good, Very Bad Day*, or Russell Hoban's *A Baby Sister for Frances*, among countless others) for its teaching potential? When our imaginations are engaged, we learn what we perhaps wouldn't, or couldn't, otherwise. Indeed, some literary critics believe that fairy tales and other classic stories from our culture's oral tradition were early forms of psychotherapy. Communities shared their wisdom, guidance and history through storytelling. Stories help us to think of opportunities for change, for acting upon our better intentions. To this end, we have included a number of stories in this book.

So, please accept these stories in this simple fashion: these are stories about people struggling with the everyday realities of their humanness, sometimes making the right choices, sometimes not. But mostly, there is some real meaty discussion and a stirring pep rally. Over the years that Madelyn has worked with parents and child educators, she has discovered a pressing need for attention to these matters of character development and integrity. Too many of us, in adapting our parenting style to the changing times, quite frankly, threw the baby out with the bath water. We cannot afford to overlook these issues; our children need us to remember that life demands that they be whole people, people who understand when their personal integrity is at risk. So, settle back into your chair, pour yourself some tea (iced in Texas with Madelyn, hot in Ontario with Vicky) and join us for a good walk through the topic.

Please keep in mind that in writing this text, we by no means suggest that we or our children are the perfect models for character and integrity. We too struggle with doing the right thing daily. These words should merely serve as a stimulus to thought and discussion on these matters.

Victoria Mathies

P.S. These stories, by the way, are fiction. Any similarity to any person, living or dead, is purely coincidental. You know the drill.

> Purposefulness requires a moral context...the construction of narratives is, therefore, a major business of our species; certainly, no group of humans has ever been found that did not have a story that defined for them how they ought to behave and why.   —Neil Postman

Table of Contents

Chapter One:
What is Good Character?

Anna had never met her grandfather in the flesh, but she could see him, standing by his locomotive in vivid color, just the same. That he had been round faced and round of body, worn a workman's boots and grimy clothing, she had learned from the pictures her grandmother had shown her on her last visit to England. But the real man, the one she could conjure up in her mind's eye had a certain distinctiveness to him; he had solidities that told her more about him than those black and white photos.

On the surface, he had been a simple man. He had started work for the steel company as a railroad worker at seventeen, hauling slag from the factory works to the man-made mountain named after him on the city's limits. He had retired at seventy-five with no company pension, just his meager savings to support him. He had been too young to go to war in the first Great War, and too old to fight in the Second. There his son had shouldered the family's burden and contribution in a bomb disposal division. Despite his absence from the front and its "glory," he'd had a solid, no nonsense approach toward life that had earned the respect and affection of neighbors and townsfolk alike.

Sitting by the radio one spring day in 1939, he'd taken the time to comfort his young, new-to-motherhood neighbor, for whom the announcement of war had made the world suddenly fall apart. He didn't shelter her, she'd told Anna; he'd told her the truth and told her, with a solid calmness to which she had clung through many dark days and even darker nights, that they would all get through this together. They would help one another. He couldn't predict the future, but they'd try to shape each day as best they could. "He was a man who knew his own worth," she had quietly told Anna, "not in that pushy way. In that simple, wise way of knowing what he could and could not do. Mr. Appleton was like that, he was." His inability to help by going to war, Anna had learned, had been translated into small actions which had much larger daily impacts. He had built, for his family and the neighbors, a bomb shelter at the end of his garden, a place lined with blue hydrangeas and pink daisies. And, at a time when children's lives were greatly restricted and burdened—gas masks, rationed food and the terror of bomb-filled nights—he'd gone to several junk yards and built from the ground up, with scrap pieces of steel piping and rubber, a tricycle for the little boys next door. They could have received no greater gift than this thoughtfulness, his knowledge of what children needed, and his willingness to spend his time making someone else's burdens easier.

Standing at the door of his wardrobe, where his suits still hung though he had been gone many years, Anna reached in and pulled toward her face the sleeve of an old tweed jacket. If there was any part of him clinging there, she could not detect it. The closet had been closed, dark and damp for too long to offer much. Closing its rickety door with a click and turning to face the stark and empty room, Anna could find nothing tangible of him remaining. He'd left her long before, and he'd left her nothing to know him by.

But no. Moving to the small leaded window of the room which overlooked the street, Anna saw the neighbors going peaceably about their day. They called to one another over their garden gates and acknowledged each other in their polite English way. No, she thought, he'd left her quite a bit: a simple life need not be unremarkable. One can still do the right thing, be a good person. She picked up the picture from the end table by the bed, the only adornment the room now held. Her grandfather stood, not quite straight, his back had seen hard labor, dressed in a dark jacket and dungarees with coal smeared across the front, the powerful engine looming large behind him. He had looked, with his pale blue eyes and white hair framing his face, cap on his head, straight into the camera. Yes, Anna thought. She had found her grandfather's inheritance here. He had been a good man; he had had character. The example of his life had been his most important gift.

What do we really want as parents? We want to love a child, have a rich family life, be part of some bigger plan than just ourselves. Yet what do we want our children to be like? Well, perfect, naturally. We want healthy, bright, creative children. We want our children to grow up well and find a purpose of their own, a successful life's work, a family, happiness. We want them to be good people, the kind of people we would want as neighbors and friends. Few of us, however, know instinctively how to make all of this happen. There are no formulas, nor guarantees, for a perfect life, at least none that I've ever heard about or discovered.

Nevertheless, what I have often struggled with as a

parent is my desire to have helped my child to become a good person. What do I mean by "good"? It's not that simple kind of good which really means "nice" in some loose and shallow kind of way. It is that other "good." I want my children to be people who know what doing the right thing means, who have the strength of their own convictions—who *have* convictions—and the personal integrity and wherewithal to act upon those convictions. In short, I want my children to have character.

Definitions of character use words like *moral excellence and firmness* or say that character is *one of the attributes or features that make up and distinguish the individual.* Character is *the complex of mental and ethical traits which marks a person, a group, a nation.* These definitions are helpful because that is exactly it; that's what I want. I want my child to have moral fiber, that sense of right and wrong which distinguishes one life from another. Like I said, I want to raise good people. In addition, I want my children to have integrity, *the ability to practice what one believes in, to be who one thinks she is and wants others to believe she is.* I want that *wholeness* that integrity can mean.

That is what this book is about. Over the twenty or more years of our deep and fulfilling friendship, Vicky and I have shared our deepest concerns, fears and aspirations for our children. We have spent hours, days, weeks, years, helping each other to be the best parent we could, and marveled at the great joys and satisfaction and challenges our children have brought to our lives. Here we'd like to share our twenty years' worth of research, conversation and debate about helping our children—and yours—to develop character and what that looks like on a daily basis.

As parents, and as a society, we need to share our thoughts about character with one another and to stimulate others to talk about these things. We need to think about what character is, what it looks like in action, and what we can do to encourage it to develop. Wanting our children to be "nice" isn't good enough. We need them—the world needs them—to do the right thing *because* it is the right thing. Perhaps then our children will live out, for themselves of course, our hopes for them. To hold down jobs our children will need to persevere and value excellence; to sustain happy marriages they will need to recognize the value of compromise, forgiveness and benevolence; to become good parents they will need to find a balance between self-sacrifice, unconditional love and self-fulfillment.

Rebellious Parents

[Parents] must conceive of parenting as an act of rebellion against culture. This is especially the case in America. For example, for parents merely to remain married is itself an act of disobedience and an insult to the spirit of a throwaway culture in which continuity has little value. It is also almost un-American to remain in close proximity to one's extended family so that children can experience, daily, the meaning of kinship and the value of deference and responsibility to elders. Similarly, to insist that one's children learn the discipline of delayed gratification, or modesty in their sexuality, or self-restraint in manners, language, and style is to place oneself in opposition to almost every social trend. But most rebellious of all is the attempt to control the media's access to one's children.[1]

When I first read these words by Neil Postman I felt a warm glow of passion flare up in me. Perhaps I should describe it as a bonfire, roaring brilliantly against a night sky. Why? Because so often over the years that I've been a parent I've felt I've been struggling against some monolithic force which I felt powerless to defeat. When my children were small and I was navigating the check out line at the grocery store, and their small eyes and hands reached out for the deliberately and strategically placed candy bars, I thought I was struggling with the children. Gradually I realized that it was the deep disrespect with which my society treated me, a mother trying to feed and care for children, that I fought. It was so inconsiderate and disrespectful for the stores I *had* to use to care so little for the importance of the job I was doing. The need for commercial success was apparently more important than children. I dealt with my children's behavior, but a small campfire began to kindle in my soul. Why should I be put in this position? Now, after reading what Mr. Postman has to say, I realize that what I felt then, and what I feel now, is rebelliousness.

I have, by being the parent I am, rebelled consistently against the forces gripping my society. I have fought, over and over again, against those forces which overtly suggest that I am taking this all too seriously: just let the child have the candy bars, watch violent movies, go to the all-night-no-parent-supervised party. Everybody else is doing it. That has never been a good enough reason for me, and it isn't for the children I care about, yours and mine. As parents, as people who are responsible one way or another, for the well-being of our families, our communities and our country, we need to be rebellious in the most positive of ways.

When everything and everybody around us tells us that our children will be fine, leave it alone, all is well, I need to remember what I want. My goal is to raise children with character. This cannot develop in a vacuum nor without planning and purposefulness. Often it seems as if the only way to ensure this will happen is to act rebelliously—*for the good of my children.*

Chapter Checkpoints

✔ Character involves having moral fiber, a sense of right and wrong that distinguishes one life from another. "Character is that within a person which governs moral choices…it is teaching the young to make wise and kind choices." —Mary Pipher

✔ Integrity is the ability to practice what we believe.

✔ Currently, we parents will frequently need to rebel and fight against our culture.

Chapter Two:
What is Important?

"Two things fill my mind with ever-increasing wonder and awe: the starry heavens above me and the moral law within me." —Immanuel Kant

"If there is anything we wish to change in the child, we should first examine it and see whether it is not something that could better be changed in ourselves." —Carl Jung

"We are the people our parents warned us about." —Jimmy Buffet

Who Really Comes First?

Let's start at the very beginning—with love. If you are taking time to read this book, it is clear that you are concerned about your children and the development of their character. It's a safe bet that you love your children and care deeply for your children's welfare. What is not so certain is how you define love, and we will need some consensus on this. The definition of love put forward in this book is the toughest I have ever encountered. I learned it from my husband: he believes that if you genuinely love someone that this means you are willing to put his or her best interests first, ahead of your own, on a regular basis, without resentment. I know this definition flies in the face of the myriad offerings of our modern self-help, self-focused society, but if most marriages operated from this definition, there would be fewer divorces, less divisiveness, maybe even more happiness. As you can see, it includes a willingness to be inconvenienced by the ones we love.

Children are immensely inconvenient. Children radically alter our lives. If they don't, there is usually something amiss—with us.

Most of us decide to have our children at moments of great optimism in our lives: we have a sense of hopefulness for ourselves, our relationships, and the future. When they come to us our children are fragile, innocent and so needy of our love and protection. As they become aware of us as separate beings, they shower us with affection—warm slobbery kisses and sticky fingers in our hair—and their new found sense of themselves—defiance, whininess, and teary demands for the impossible. It is easy for us to mistake their need of us for deep and abiding love, but it is not. Don't misunderstand me: it *is* love. Still, it is not the love of a mature adult whose decision to love is freely given and chosen. It is the love of a child. Our children are bound to us by the complicated web of family loyalty, need for protection and force of habit. It is not a certainty that they will come to love us in any kind of special way. Certainly it will never be the way in which we love and cherish them. And that, I believe, is what sets parents, especially good parents, apart from all other caretakers, indeed all other relationships. The transaction is, as it must be, singularly one-sided. We love them; perhaps one day they will *come to love us.* We cannot, as parents, expect our children to fill our needs for reciprocated love and affection. As adults we must get our needs for these met elsewhere.

That is not to say that our children don't teach us a great deal about love. Most of us find our love affair with our first child huge and overwhelming. The world feels both wonderful and terrifyingly dangerous simultaneously. One mother described her first few seconds of parenthood as being bittersweet, realizing the joy of a new life and the potential for pain all in the same second. Where before she had felt certain and confident and competent in her life, she now felt a little more vulnerable. And in the days preceding the birth of her second child, she felt grief and loss for that wonderful feeling she felt for her oldest. She was afraid that she could never love another child as she loved the first. It had seemed a miracle then when the second was born, and looking down into that tiny face, she realized that her love had no particular limits. She loved the second as fiercely and strongly as she had the first. Her love could and would stretch and grow to include another.

That, it seems, is the challenge. As parents we must find a way to take our rather ordinary skins and stretch them to capacity, fill them with our potential to love. It is only with our love that we can find the courage to do the job as it needs doing. Guiding, supporting, teaching, pushing, protecting, cherishing...these tasks both exhaust, enrich and change our lives forever. Being a parent can be one of the most, if not the most, demanding exercises in our own character development.

Love is about *them*, not about *us*. Loving your children, then, means providing them with what they need. Please note a distinction here: this does not mean that we must provide them with what they want. Indeed, giving them all they want will hinder their character development. Needing and wanting are two entirely different concepts. Loving a child, that is to say, choosing to look after her best interests, means saying "no cookies before dinner" and sticking to it. Giving in to a distressed or argumentative child may be easier in the short term for us, but this is most certainly not in the best interest of the child's nutrition or character development. Nor does this qualify as good parenting or discipline. Devaluing yourself and going into servitude to your children is not being suggested. I would never recommend this; a child can and should usually wait on himself. If he wants the mustard, you do not need to fetch it for him; he needs to learn how to get it for himself, and he needs the opportunity to discover he can rely on himself. When we give everything to our children and do everything for them, we devalue ourselves to nothing more than their servants. In so doing, we deny them the opportunity to develop the self-regard and character which come with providing service to themselves and to others.

Children need so much. They have physical needs for food, shelter, and clothing; they must be protected from a host of dangers. They need nurturing and emotional support, and they need parents who are prepared to guide, teach and discipline them. In short, they need parents who will prepare them for the world outside the walls of home. A child's needs tend to be immediate, constant, and continual. I have yet to meet a parent who was not at times worn out and overwhelmed by a single child, let alone two or three. Nor have I met the "natural" parent, one whose parenting capacity and skills seem innate. There are birth parents, adoptive parents, and stepparents but no natural parents. We will all be struggling and building character along this journey.

Nothing in my life has given me more pain than being a mother. I hasten to add that nothing has given me more joy either. I need to be clear: the children did not cause me the pain. I was the cause of my own pain. Nothing in my life has forced me to address my greatest weaknesses the way being a parent has. No college course, job or friend—not even my husband—was enough to make me identify my weaknesses, let alone face them and deal with them. My children were the single prime motivators in this large step towards personal growth. My children have taught me courage. Rooting out my weaknesses, like selfishness, greed and disrespect, has not been easy. But in the end, I am a much better person, *with more character,* than I would have been had I not had children. Our children can teach us a great deal if we are open and willing; some of the hardest won, but best parts of ourselves, are owed to our relationship with them. I owe my children a great deal. Nonetheless, it was at times a very difficult and painful journey.

Love means a willingness to sacrifice, but in a wise and purposeful way. Rest assured I'm not even remotely suggesting martyrdom, though the job is vexing and can be exhausting. I am suggesting that it is other-serving, not self-serving. We had these children because we sought to love. Falling in love is easy; that is about our own senses and the joy in their being alive. Being *in love* is easy; *loving prudently* is hard. Holding onto this love, on a daily and moment to moment basis, now that's the struggle. Clichéd and idealistic as it was, in the sixties there was a lot of talk about love being a verb, not a noun. For parents, love must be a verb. "When you believe that 'the family comes first for me,' everything else follows."[2] You must believe and act on this. Who but a parent could or would?

Love, then, is something either you understand and practice or you don't. If you don't, the job of parenting, let alone developing character in your children, won't get done. It's too difficult, too intense and too constant. Without love, we simply are not up to the task. Period.

As he gazed around the dusk-lit room, he felt a wave of cold terror seize him. Beside the closet on a wooden giraffe, hung a rag-tag assortment of clothing, which in the growing darkness was bit by bit transforming itself into something far more sinister. In daylight, the nursery wallpaper sported a series of bright blue and red dancing bears; in the encroaching gloom they leapt off the wall as disfigured and unrecognizable creatures of varying size. Kyle's small stomach began to churn and he clutched his nighttime companion, Fuzzy, close to his chest. Sweat beaded up on his forehead and as a whispering fear crept further into his extremities, his ankles, toes and fingers buzzed and tingled out of control. When he heard the scream, he had no idea where it had come from, certainly could not have placed it as coming from himself.

Mommy, arriving swiftly but bleary-eyed to his side, pulled him close and smoothed away the dark loneliness of the room. "Ssshh...sweetheart. I'm here," she whispered, pressing his warm, damp head close to hers. She kissed his curls and savored the soft scent only he possessed. "Don't cry. There's nothing to be afraid of."

The child clung tightly, his body relaxing only in the smallest amount. He sobbed, words garbled by the choking in his throat, "But, Mommy, it's dark. There's something going to get me. Don't leave, don't leave."

As she rocked his shivery body gently, she said, "Sweetheart, I want you to listen very carefully. Mommy and Daddy love you very, very much. We wouldn't let you sleep where it was dangerous. We only ever allow you to be where it is safe. So," she said, looking him straight in the face, "when you are alone and afraid I want you to tell yourself—in fact, I want you to tell Fuzzy and the entire room—you shout it: I'm safe in my room. I'm safe in my room."

Kyle thought about that. In the light he knew the truth of these words; in the dark it was an entirely different matter. As his tears subsided, a quiet fatigue settled into his legs and arms, making him feel heavy and motionless. Mommy tucked him in, pulling the blankets up to his chin and tucking Fuzzy close to his chest under one lethargic arm. Saying goodnight she kissed both their ears, first one then the other, and their various smooth and fuzzy foreheads. Moments later she slid soundlessly from the room.

Fuzzy fell asleep; Kyle, with a small boy's determination to fight off a tide of sleepy waves, kept his eyes open, alert to all potential danger. As the panicky feeling began again in his stomach, he tried to remember what Mommy had said. You're safe, she'd said. We love you and we wouldn't let you sleep where it wasn't safe. Shout that to the room. His voice, small and quavery at first, but becoming more confident said, "Mommy and Daddy love me and I'm safe. I'm safe, I'm safe...I'M SAFE!" Despite the silence his declaration received from the room, he leaned back into the pillow and joined Fuzzy in sleep. When Mommy looked in five minutes later, his body had relaxed into a calm slumber. He slept safe, secure, and certainly, loved.

Chapter Checkpoints
✔ Loving our children is the first and most basic step. To truly love means to put their best interest before our own. This is not easy, but essential to the development of good character.
✔ Raising children with character builds our own character—with pain and over time.

Chapter Three:
Touchstones

There are three concepts or touchstones which we will return to frequently in this book. These three touchstones, Finding Happiness, Making Connection, and Doing the Right Thing, are essential building blocks in the formation of good character and the cultivation of integrity. In fact, if we allow ourselves to think of these three touchstones as the outermost points of an equilateral triangle, we can see how each is a prerequisite and building block for the other. Making strong Connections with others helps us to Find Happiness and ensures that we feel in our lives the need to Do the Right Thing. Similarly, Doing the Right Thing often helps us to Make Connections with others and consequently to Find Happiness. Or, in Finding some inner Happiness, we are open to Making important Connections in our lives and empowered to Do the Right Thing. Entering the triangle and moving in any direction will move us to a place that will improve the quality of our lives and that of those around us.

Finding Happiness

Making Connections   Doing the Right Thing

It is also true that if we leave out any point on the triangle, then the triangle's integrity—and, that is to say, our moral integrity—may also be compromised. These points or touchstones are mutually dependent.

Finding Happiness

In his book *The Art of Happiness,*[3] the Dalai Lama asserts that the purpose of life is to seek happiness. Surely no one would argue that this is an important goal of our life here on earth. We must be quite specific, however, about what is meant by happiness since confusion about it abounds. Here in North America, we tend to think that anyone seeking happiness would lead a self-centered and self-indulgent life. In truth, unhappy people tend to be more self-focused and to feel self-important. Happy people, by contrast, are more sociable, outer- and other-focused, loving and forgiving.

So what am I trying to get at here? Until we have a measure of contentedness and satisfaction in our lives, it is very difficult for us to focus on doing the right thing. In fact, our unhappy strivings are blocks to our seeing what is the right thing to do. For example, finding happiness cannot derive from simply getting what we want. Similarly, whether we will be happy or unhappy can generally be predicted by whether the objects of our desire are positive or negative. How one tells whether a desire is positive or negative is not by whether it gives one an immediate sense of satisfaction but by whether its consequences are ultimately positive or negative. Many vices, such as lying, stealing, cheating or overeating are immediately gratifying. Their long-term effects are negative. A supreme interest of our culture at the present moment, for example, is the accumulation of material things, or conspicuous consumption. If we get a new car or re-carpet the stairs or outfit ourselves in new clothes, then we will be happy. But do these purchases really affect or change who we are? Some of us are never satisfied with what we have and need always to collect more. Contentment then is the cure for consumption and greed. If one is truly content, then it matters not at all whether one acquires another object. As long as we are busy acquiring, we may ignore doing the right thing and overlook making connections.

Nor can true happiness come from gratification of the senses alone. Indeed, since we cannot permanently gratify our senses, we can only appease them temporarily. A glass of water when we are thirsty satisfies, but only for a time; too much water bloats us and causes us discomfort.[4]

Clearly, we need to find a more lasting and enduring variety of happiness for ourselves, some inner contentedness that allows us to consider the needs of others and to choose to act ethically *simply because it is the right thing to do.*

Abundance

The principle component of happiness is a genuine sense of contentment and well-being. Once developed, our changing circumstances have very little effect on it. We all know people who seem blessed with abundance of spirit, outlook and generosity. These people seem to have an abundance, not of material things necessarily, but of emotional and mental well-being. They feel not only that they have enough, but that there is enough to go around. Because these people feel content, they often feel able to share their compassion, resources and moral leadership with others.

By contrast, many of us experience a feeling of scarcity; we feel that there is very little of what we need going around and that we will likely be unable to grasp hold of any, let alone enough. We are always waiting for the other shoe to drop. Our glasses are half empty, not half full. I believe that our inborn temperaments have something to do with this; our negative life experiences can also contribute. We are not locked into this world view. We can retool and consciously seek a change in our ability to see more potential in others and in ourselves. We can also help our children to do this.

If we allow ourselves to dwell on negative thoughts and emotions, we may find it hard work to be happy and to act ethically. When we feel that what we need is scarce, it is easier for us to lack compassion and act selfishly. We feel that we don't have much to share. If we don't find a way to fill our lives with a sense of contentedness, then we will be unable to tap into a wellspring of ethical behavior and character.

Negative Thoughts

This is not to say that we can never harbor negative thoughts or feelings. Consider anger as an example. Although righteous anger at an injustice can cause ethical behavior, much of our anger is destructive. It destroys our compassion toward others and frequently is caused by taking other people's actions too personally, especially our children's. When we respond to the need for problem solving with anger, we very often cannot find the solutions we need; instead we can do damage to others and ourselves. I am not suggesting that we should deny or suppress our emotions; this is unhealthy. We need, rather, to reduce the number of issues that we allow ourselves to become angry or upset about; we must control our feelings, rather than let them control us and lead us astray. To paraphrase Eleanor Roosevelt, no one can make you mad without your permission.[5]

Happiness, inner peace, tranquility, contentment, whatever we choose to call it, is the first touchstone. In direct opposition are negative feelings—anger, discontentment, envy, greed, and scarcity. Happiness includes a sense of abundance and compassion; it leads to ethical behavior and good character. This touchstone clearly adds to our willingness to contribute to another's happiness and to look after another's interests (love) as well as our own. It is a direct link, of course, to the second touchstone, Making Connection.

Making Connection

Making Connection involves demonstrating a genuine concern for others, an ability to reach out to them and to understand them. Sometimes we are more familiar with disconnection. Disconnection is "a moment when the people involved experience the pain of not being understood and of not understanding the other person. Disconnections are what we experience when we feel cut off from those with whom we share a relationship."[6]

Arriving at the dock after three days of rainy paddling, Annaliese felt the anxiety in her chest deepen. She had been paddling head down, eyes closed, and with her mind anywhere but huddled in the damp and cold canoe. Since she felt she must set a good example for the girls she was counselor to, she had paddled with a dogged determination trying to keep going, despite the nausea, the loneliness and the numbness of her arms and legs.

The dock was gray with age and rotting at the edges. It dipped into the water at its far edge like a shovel in sand. It was more a ramp than a functional dock. A path led from the dock to a small variety store on the far side of the railway tracks; the girls from her canoe ran cheerfully along it. Walking along the path took you from the sickly sweet smell of overly wet vegetation to the heavy smell of creosoted railway timbers and, finally, to the small, musty cabin where you could buy milk, candy bars, white bread, chips and a few junky magazines. The woman behind the counter was not what you would call friendly, but not unfriendly either. She didn't have much to say to these soggy lake travelers. The girls bought candy bars and chewing gum, their laughter filling every small space of the store; Annaliese stood numbly by, taking none of her usual delight in chocolate and sweets.

To the left of the store, there was, she saw, a red and black plastic telephone booth. Miraculously, here was a lifeline. Without even a second thought she walked the short distance to the booth. She pressed zero and waited for the operator.

"I'd like to place a collect call, please," she told the operator. "The area code is 505 and the number is 381-9614. My name is Annaliese."

Her mother's voice as she accepted the charges was tentative; clearly this was not what she'd expected when she picked up the phone. "Hi, dear," she said. "Where are you?"

"A place called Kiosk on North Tea Lake, I think."

"Ahhh...why are you calling? Everything okay?"

"Well, I don't know...it's just that I'm tired and sick and, ummm...I just thought I'd call," Annaliese whispered, groping for the meaning of this reaching out. Why had she called? What could her mother do at this distance?

"Well, there's nothing new going on here; you're not missing a thing," her mother replied cheerily. "How are Penny and Maria?"

"They're not on this trip, Mum. It's the other counselor, Ingrid and I, and six girls."

"Oh...I see. And how's your weather? We're having glorious sunny summer days. Just perfect, really."

Annaliese could no longer think of what to say. Here she was beside a grubby northern pitstop, a black painted garbage barrel overflowing incongruously beside the pristine velvety brown lake. It was drizzling unmercifully. Certain suddenly that at these prime time prices there was no conversation worth having, she said goodbye and hung up. The girls' purchases made, she walked with them back to the path, back over the creosoted timbers and down to the mossy, rotting dock and into the blue canoe. Here, at least, she felt at home.

As they headed back out into the late afternoon light of the lake, she bent her head again and lowered her shoulder. She straightened her lower arm and allowed herself to be swept up again into the rhythm of paddling. Dip, stroke, lift and swing. Dip, stroke, lift and swing. Trance-like she watched the eddies created by the paddle's movement in the water. A tight anxiety clutched at her chest again. Closing her eyes she allowed the rhythm of the steady paddling movement to wash over her. Dip, stroke, lift and swing. Dip, stroke, lift and swing.

Disconnection happens when we fail to listen and fail to demonstrate understanding of what is being shared or when we fail to be honest and direct about our own feelings. In the above story, what would have happened if Annaliese's mother had really listened, had really connected with her daughter? She would have helped to grow the bond between them; instead, she put distance between them and caused her daughter pain rather than relieving it. "A painful moment of disconnection might have been transformed into a powerful moment of connection."[7] Making Connection with others is a key ingredient in intimacy, a major component in any healthy relationship.

> Our fundamental notions of who we are are not formed in the process of separation from others, but within the mutual interplay of relationships with others. In short, the goal is not for the individual to grow out of relationships, but to grow into them. As the relationships grow, so grows the individual. Participating in growth-fostering relationships is both the source and the goal of development.[8]

How well we are connected to others depends much on how we perceive them. This has much to do with what goes on inside ourselves. If we are trustworthy and honest, we are more likely to view others as being trustworthy. Similarly, if we lie regularly, we tend to distrust others more. If we view others as wanting connection, having abundance, wanting to do the right thing, we are more likely to form beneficial and life affirming relationships with them, relationships where empathy flows and our mutual interest connects us. It is through these connections that we find ourselves wanting to act in another's best interests. And here we are, back to the importance of love and its close association to our sense of well-being.

On the other hand, if our relationships are not based upon empathic connection and love, but rather upon a "what can I get out of this" attitude, the focus of our behavior is not mutual benefit, but immediate self-gratification. An inflated sense of our own entitlement coupled with our need for immediate self-gratification, allow us to disrespect and violate the rights of others.

Empathy

Empathy is a key ingredient in connection. It is the ability to suspend your own viewpoint and put yourself in someone else's shoes, to try to view a situation from the other's perspective and to determine what you would think, feel and do in his place. It is not so easy as it sounds. First turning down and off our own perspective is very difficult. We are, after all, so very right in our views; they wouldn't be our views if they weren't right! When we can silence our perspective and make the leap into another's paradigm, empathy takes place. With empathy comes compassion, *a deep awareness of the suffering of another coupled with the wish to relieve it.*[9] Compassion is a first step to connection. Once truly aware of each other, we recognize that we have many commonalities. Compassion springs from our genuine understanding of this fact.

With our concern for others, we can focus less on our own worries and concerns and reduce our experience of our own stress. The more concerned we are with others, the less preoccupied we are with ourselves. The more we develop compassion for others, the more ethical our behavior will become. When we act out of concern for others, out of compassion, we create peace in ourselves, which often we are able to generate outwardly toward others. For example, when we have abundance and balance in our lives, equanimity follows, and we respond differently to our children's misbehavior; we handle it better and have a chance at generating peace. My friend Julie told me about her nephew Zak who was grabbing candy in the grocery store. Julie called to him twice to get his attention, but he did not stop nor respond in any way. She went to him, put the candy back, and told him it was time to leave the store. He immediately dropped into a lump. Knowing she was about to enter a power struggle she could easily lose (Zak is 60 pounds of muscle, sinew, and determination), she changed tactics. She looked him straight in the eye and said, "I'll race you back to your Mom, and I bet I can beat you." Off Zak ran, without a struggle. Julie's empathy for Zak and his situation (very much wanting the candy) and her ability to touch calmness rather than get irritated, allowed her to change tactics and spread peace. The benefits to parents of trying to develop and maintain a reserve of tranquility cannot be overstated. Children, especially the very young and the teenaged, test our patience, forbearance, and tranquility on a frequent and regular basis. This is part of their job as our children. Whenever we can find calm and compassion, we handle ourselves, our children, and our problems better and our modeling of conduct under pressure is helpful and positive to our children.

Inner worth is a result of having an internal source of happiness and contentment. No matter what has happened to us, as long as we know we can relate to others because we are each human, we share a bond, a connection. It is this connection that gives rise to a sense of dignity and worth and to consolation, even if we lose almost everything else—body functions, spouse, job, eyesight, status, house or possessions. Without a feeling of connection or affection for others, life can be difficult indeed and certainly more difficult than it need be. Only a person with a sense of connection and worth based on his relationships with others can afford to lose other things—health, wealth and security, which unfortunately, are always at risk, and never guaranteed.

Doing the Right Thing

It sounds so simple, so clear. Just choose to do the right thing and you will be a person of character. Yet, choosing to do the right thing is difficult much of the time for any number of different reasons. Why don't we choose to eat only foods which are good for us? Why don't we exercise daily as we know we should? Why don't we let a waiting car into traffic? Let alone the big issues. Why do we yell at our most precious people, our children and our spouses? Why do we lie and cheat? We all know better. Knowledge does not translate directly and immediately into action, not for children and sadly, not for adults. What if we all followed the Golden Rule, do unto others as you would have them do unto you? Life would be better. But still we don't. We seem to share at times a disturbing lack of concern for consequences as well as a scarcity of compassion. We usually pay a price for this. So, too, do those around us.

Each day we come up against any number of choices. We do not always choose to do the right thing; all too frequently the right choice is the difficult one and often involves more inconvenience and less pleasure for us. Clearly, pleasure in and of itself is not negative. Pleasure can be derived from a sunrise, a child's giggle, a husband's kiss. It can also be derived from overeating, cocaine, and the rush which comes from physically besting or even hurting someone. We must frame our decisions about our behavior on obtaining long-term happiness not on gaining short-term pleasure. This is only prudent. In this manner, we do not give up anything we cannot afford to sacrifice long term. Ultimately, we must ask ourselves if a choice is harmful to me or beneficial to me? To others? Interestingly, if it is harmful to others, it will, in the end, also be harmful to me. It is difficult at times to remember that we are simply choosing to do the *right* thing. It is right for us as well. The secret to happiness does rest within our own hands.

Self-discipline

At first thought, it would seem that if we all naturally seek happiness, that we would quite easily, if not far more easily, seek to do the right things. Yet time and again, we watch ourselves and others fail to do this. Often this can be the result of choosing immediate gratification over deferred gratification. After all, when a temptation is right there in front of us, the urge to succumb can be very strong. The shoes we do not need are beautiful and would look stunning with a dress we already own; the rich dessert smells wonderful; away from home and spouse, we discover that the good-looking woman is attracted to us too. We even warn ourselves, "I know I shouldn't but...." It takes a great deal of self-discipline not to indulge in unwholesome but immediately pleasurable temptations. Developing self-discipline can be the work of a lifetime; maintaining it always is. Self-discipline can and does slip quickly away for just the moment it takes to falter. We must train ourselves, and we must stay vigilant.

One problem with our current society is that we have an attitude towards education as if it is there to simply make you more clever, make you more ingenious.... Even though our society does not emphasize this, the most important use of knowledge and education is to help us understand the importance of engaging in more wholesome actions and bringing about discipline within our minds. The proper utilization of our intelligence and knowledge is to effect changes from within to develop a good heart.[10]

> "It is only with the heart that one can see rightly; what is essential is invisible to the eye." —Antoine de Saint-Exupéry, *The Little Prince*

Standing on the court, sweat dripping from his brow and the tip of his nose, salty and hot, he was pushed by the opposing team's guard from behind. Turning to see who had shoved him, he was greeted with the caustic sounds of hatred and anger in the other boy's voice. "*#@!," the boy spat at him, his face mottled red with rage. Riley was only momentarily stunned; playing basketball he'd seen quite a variety of sportsmanship these last few months. Some teams fastidiously played fair and retained on-court composure; others shouted and complained at every call and wore faces lined with anxiety and frustration.

Today's game was fast paced, the players moving up and down the court at breakneck speed. As Riley reached and maintained his position under the net, he jumped up to block the other boy's shot, receiving a vicious blow to the ribs and a stream of foul language for his efforts. Shaking it off as best he could, he looked briefly at the other player wondering what was wrong with him. "Are you okay?" he inquired. There was no response. The other boy's team was winning easily; the game was theirs, not much to worry about.

Five minutes later he would block yet another shot, feeling a surge of adrenaline rush through his arms and legs. He felt hot and cold at the same time. Even losing the game couldn't rob him of his satisfaction in his own day's performance. A curly headed boy, the player guarding him this quarter, turned to him with a smile and said, "Great block. You've made some good blocks." Riley, surprised, smiled back, saying, "Thanks." A soft warmth spread across his chest. The two stood amiably together for a second until play resumed.

What makes one child vicious, foul and unkind under pressure, and another gracious, admiring and friendly? How does a third player continue to find tremendous satisfaction in the play, allowing such invective and hostility to slide right off him?

Hatred, jealousy, anger, even irritation are negative states of emotion. They destroy happiness and connection with others. They generate fear, isolation, insecurity, and disconnection. They also allow us more easily to choose to do the wrong things.

We must develop spiritual discipline or self-discipline with regard to our emotions. Knowing that anger or jealousy is destructive does not guard against their arrival. We cannot simply force ourselves not to feel this way; we must understand how and why these emotions are destructive to ourselves and to others. We must be aware of their destructive nature and ward against them. We must recognize their imminence and learn to diffuse or disarm them.

Clearly we must not only reduce our negative emotions and thoughts, we must also cultivate positive thoughts, feelings and actions. Forbearance, *tolerance and restraint in the face of provocation and patience* will be required.[11] Negative emotions, those which are self-serving not other-serving include anger, greed, lust, pride, and hatred. They cause anxiety, stress, and confusion, and they are called vices. They can be the cause of unethical and wrong behavior. As stated earlier, they also interfere with both tranquility and connection. They allow us to become insensitive or oblivious to the impact of our behavior on others. They allow us to cease seeking others' happiness. This, in turn, allows for our own disconnection and loss of happiness. They are inextricably bound. When we choose to do wrong, we cannot feel all "right" with ourselves. We must over time and with effort develop other means of responding to adverse and averse situations.

We must all look deeply into ourselves and find what prevents us from doing the right thing and allows us to do wrong. It is easier to understand why our children do wrong. They have so many lessons to learn, and their misbehavior guides us to their needed lesson. Perhaps we grownups are still in process, still somewhat uncivilized, and still have lessons to learn as well. But when does the statute of limitations run out? When do we put aside our emotional baggage? When must we "cowboy up" and be responsible? When do missed lessons become stupidity on our parts? I wish I had those answers. I do know that if you are a parent, it is time. You are being watched and are affecting not simply your own life but another's, your child's. Your time has come whether you are ready or not. As Margaret Anderson stated so sagely, "The struggle with moral perfection ends only at the grave."[12] She's right. And it is time to struggle mightily and win, or at least come very close.

> Our children do not need perfect parents. They need parents who strive for integrity and moral ideals; who make mistakes but learn from them; who will share their principles, struggles and thoughts with their children; and, who put their children first, in practice not just in thought. We need to handle our lives and our children with integrity. By integrity I mean not just the ability to say what we believe but the ability to practice what we believe and the ability to do the right thing.[13]

The three touchstones then are: 1)Finding Happiness or inner peace, 2)Making Connection, empathy and mutuality with others, and 3)Doing the Right Thing. These ingredients must be present in order to have good character and to teach it. These three are tightly tied to one another. To review, contentment allows compassion for others which leads to choosing to do the right thing which, in its turn, contributes to our having more happiness. These three touchstones will be interwoven into the ideas and strategies in this text. Failing to develop any one of these touchstones will render us ineffective at, if not incapable of, helping our children develop strong character. Working on and developing these touchstones comprise our first steps in building our own integrity and character so that we are able to facilitate their growth in our children.

One afternoon Shaya and his father walked past a park where some boys Shaya knew were playing baseball. Shaya asked, "Do you think they will let me play?" Shaya's father knew that his son was not at all athletic and that most boys would not want him on their team. But Shaya's father understood that if his son was chosen to play it would give him a comfortable sense of belonging. Shaya's father approached one of the boys in the field and asked if Shaya could play. The boy looked around for guidance from his teammates. Getting none, he took matters into his own hands and said, "We are losing by six runs and the game is in the eighth inning. I guess he can be on our team, and we'll try to put him up to bat in the ninth inning." Shaya's father was ecstatic as Shaya smiled broadly.

Shaya was told to put on a glove and go out to play short center field. In the bottom of the eighth inning, Shaya's team scored a few runs but was still behind by three. In the bottom of the ninth inning, Shaya's team scored again and now with two outs and the bases loaded with the potential winning run on base, Shaya was scheduled to be up. Would the team actually let Shaya bat at this juncture and give away their chance to win the game? Surprisingly, Shaya was given the bat. Everyone knew that it was all but impossible because Shaya didn't even know how to hold the bat properly, let alone hit with it. However, as Shaya stepped up to the plate, the pitcher moved in a few steps to lob the ball in softly so Shaya should at least be able to make contact.

The first pitch came in and Shaya swung clumsily and missed. One of Shaya's teammates came up to Shaya and together they held the bat and faced the pitcher waiting for the next pitch. The pitcher again took a few steps forward to toss the ball softly toward Shaya. As the pitch came in, Shaya and his teammate swung the bat and together they hit a slow ground ball to the pitcher. The pitcher picked up the soft grounder and could easily have thrown the ball to the first baseman. Shaya would have been out and that would have ended the game; the pitcher paused for a moment.

Instead, the pitcher took the ball and threw it on a high arc to right field, far beyond reach of the first baseman. Everyone started yelling, "Shaya, run to first. Run to first!" Never in his life had Shaya run to first. He scampered down the baseline wide-eyed and startled. By the time he reached first base, the right fielder had the ball. He could have thrown the ball to the second baseman who would tag out Shaya, who was still running. But the right fielder understood what the pitcher's intentions were, so he threw the ball high and far over the third baseman's head. Everyone yelled, "Run to second, run to second." Shaya ran towards second base as the runners ahead of him deliriously circled the bases towards home. As Shaya reached second base, the opposing shortstop ran to him, turned him in the direction of third base and shouted, "Run to third." As Shaya rounded third, the boys from both teams ran behind him screaming, "Shaya run home!" Shaya ran home, stepped on home plate and all 18 boys lifted him on their shoulders and made him the hero, as he had just hit "a grand slam" and had won the game for his team.

Based on a story by Rabbi Paysach Krohn[14]

I don't know who "got" to these boys. I don't know who taught them such principles, such character. I do know someone did. Why is it that this story is so touching? Yes, the boys selflessly chose to do the right thing; their kindness and generosity of spirit is noteworthy. But the truth is, nowadays, this story seems almost impossible. What pitcher would throw away a game for another boy's happiness? I don't know, but

I want him to marry my daughter, or I want him to be my son's friend. I want to know him. This is who I want my child to be like.

Chapter Checkpoints

✔ Finding Happiness: a sense of abundance coupled with compassion for others based on our empathy and commonalities. Think twice about when and why you get angry.

✔ Making Connection: the ability to reach out to and understand others dependent upon how we perceive ourselves and how we perceive them. Mutuality and reciprocal empathy are the desired results.

✔ Doing the Right Thing: we all know and recognize "right actions"; choosing them on a regular basis requires a great deal of self-discipline and maturity. Practicing integrity, choosing to be who we wish to be, is key. Self-discipline is essential.

Chapter Four:
Misconceptions

Outside the classroom window Jenny could see large fluffy flakes of snow falling densely onto the landscaped bushes, cement curb and parking lot. The sky was uniformly grey, thick clouds heavy with snow ready to fall. Inside the classroom it was warm; the walls were littered with bright colorful posters and the class's art projects adorned the bulletin boards in preparation for the upcoming Parent's night. But inside there was noise. Always there was noise. People scraped their chairs, shouted, cursed, sharpened pencils, dropped things. Sometimes Jenny thought she would scream if there wasn't silence or just a little bit of quiet thinking time.

Mr. Kendrick, the teacher, was not what she had expected. Not that she knew what to expect really. He was new; the problems with this class weren't. This class had always had behavior problems, each year the same back-talk, shoving and disorderly disobedience. Mr. Kendrick, although he seemed firm and determined, was having no easier time than Ms. Clarke, nor Miss Carlotti for that matter, and everyone had thought her a witch. It was just plain hard to live each day in this room.

Her desire to be out in the cool, refreshing snow crowded out Jenny's desire for music and writing her letters. Outside seemed so peaceful. As she turned to face the room, she saw that there was trouble brewing. Mr. Kendrick had promised he would read their whole group the story aloud if there was quiet. "Boys, boys," he cried, "please take your seats so we can get started." As usual, he was ignored. "BOYS. Find your seats; everyone else is waiting," he said with increasing impatience, trying to exert control over the room.

To Jenny's way of thinking it was a hopeless cause: Jeremy and Marcus had begun a game of tag under the art project table, which involved a lot of bumping, shouting and cries of "you idiot," or "you're a retard." They showed no signs of having heard the request, let alone inclination to follow it. Jenny sat, her shoulders slumping, hands holding the weight of her head, and trying to will them silently away, gone, dead if necessary. She had been loving the story; she loved all stories. If only she could be in that imaginary world, flying away, away from here, from this. This chaos that was Balsam Public School's Grade Three class.

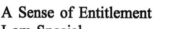

A Sense of Entitlement
I am Special

Sometimes I ask a group of parents, "Do you want your child to feel she is special?" They invariably answer that they do. This is misguided. Allow yourself to be shocked, but think a bit about why I am suggesting that this is misguided. Your child is unique and individual, but not special, except of course to you. Whoa now: hear me out. First, we have programs in our schools which make posters for each child with all of the reasons he is special. These reasons generally include: I am special because I can play video games or because I like to watch television. These posters suggest that a child is special because she is a consumer, not a producer. With these posters, specialness and self-esteem are built not on competence, good relationships with peers, productivity or even on being alive, but on the level of one's consumerism.

These projects promote narcissism, *excessive admiration for oneself or conceit,* not healthy self-esteem.

Second, do we even want our children to believe they are special? No, we don't. And don't for a moment think that all of our children can be special. By definition, we cannot all be special, most of us have to be average or regular. Unique and individual we are, and these are helpful things to teach children. Special, however, connotes something above, something better. Herein lies the problem. Think about this for a moment. We currently seem to have a problem in our society: we have too many people who believe they are entitled to any and every service and product, and further, more entitled than anyone else. They should be waited upon first; they needn't speak politely; they can interrupt whomever they please and make demands; they will accept another person's help, opening a door for instance, without a smile or a glance. These people are so special that they are entitled to interrupt a speaker, a restaurant's quiet, or a symphony's beauty with their important cell phone calls. Believing I am special would mean that I'm entitled to do all of these things and more. Wait. If I believe I am special, I am, logically, better than you. But am I? No. Yet if I am actively taught that I am special, I may believe this to be true. Let me further illustrate this point. As we drove to a seminar in Philadelphia, I watched a car blatantly and belatedly run a red light. The woman in the car with me immediately commented, "He must be special." Indeed, this driver was special, so special that he did not have to stop for a red light. For many people special can include above the law, beyond the rules and exempt from courtesy. That may not be what you want for your child, but it is all too often the end result of being special.

Yes, your child is special *to you,* but that is different from special in general and to everyone. What if we replaced special with the fact that all of our children are precious beyond belief and incredibly valuable? We have something better than special; we have priceless. Here we maintain our equality, for which child is not precious and valuable? After all, it was our founding fathers who taught us that "all men are created equal." Perhaps we need to remember this with regard not only to just under the law but with regard to the treatment of each other. We are all worthy of being treated with dignity, respect and kindness. In fact, if we are to treat each other with dignity and respect, none of us can be more special than another. My guess is that in these times where good, solid character can be difficult to find, people with this type of strong character may rank as special. They never, however, believe themselves to be special or above others. Humility is a virtue.

The children who understand this best are the very children we label *special*. Special needs children, any child with special challenges, wish to be anything *but* special. They want only to be like other children. Special needs children understand this concept early in their lives. Being special can cause disconnection with others.

Standing in the cafeteria grill line, Sharon was contentedly replaying the day. The line was slow moving however, and she had been standing on too-tired feet for fifteen minutes already. A whisper of a headache was starting at the base of her skull, and she needed to sit and rest. But, life is about lining up and waiting. Hurry up, hurry up and wait.

"Hey, Sharon. What's up?" Mike said, walking over to stand in front of her in line. Maria, Cal and Jason followed suit, until Sharon and the long line of other patient students behind her were now even further behind and further from lunch.

"Hey to you too," she replied, and added: "You don't really think you're going to stay here do you?" She folded her arms in front of her; any humor the day had left her was gone, flown away on a wind of annoyance.

"What? Come on! You mean we can't stand here with you? Don't be ridiculous," Cal said, smirking at the line behind her.

"No," Sharon said. "No way. You will need to go to the end of the line. Everyone else, including me, has already waited a long time. You will need to do so as well."

"Aw, come on. What's wrong with you tonight? Everybody does this, Sharon. Why are you being so unreasonable? No one behind you cares," Mike whined, hoping to appeal to her friendship and loyalty.

"No way. How do you know they don't care? *You* don't care about *them*. This is the whole problem with this campus, this world in fact." She was really on a roll now. "Why do you think that you have more rights, are more entitled to eat, than the rest of us here? This is a huge problem: this blatant and rampant sense of entitlement. It makes people think that they have the right to step to the front of the line, weave in and out in traffic, run red lights, and just generally run rough shod over other people and their rights."

But Sharon was talking to herself. The group stood stubbornly ahead of her in line and laughed at her. How could she be so silly? "Relax, you're just having a bad day," they said. "Chill out. Don't make such a big deal out of such a small thing."

Red rage welled up behind her eyes. Now she was upset; what had merely been a normal day's fatigue was rapidly transforming into indignation and shame. She struggled to maintain control: how could she be accused of being unreasonable when she had done nothing besides remind them of what constituted good manners? And she felt ashamed: she couldn't believe that her friends, *her friends*, and obviously the bulk of her peers, had no sense of how to treat others with respect. They seemed rarely to consider the impact of their actions on others, and they didn't care if they inconvenienced other people with their noise, their garbage or their demands. She didn't see enough people hold doors for others, offer assistance, speak with respect to sales clerks, or even cross the street without assuming that the traffic should stop. It seemed, at this moment, a huge and overwhelming societal problem.

"Look, guys," she repeated, "you'll have to go to the back of the line. You don't have the right to butt in. If you had gone when I first suggested it, you would not have had to wait so long. Talk to you later."

The gang stared at her in disbelief and then, with grinning faces walked away, and in mocking undertones described her in the most unflattering of ways. Sharon, weary and heart-sore, stood her ground. Some days it seemed you had to take on the world. The pain at the base of her skull spread, but despite the dull throb she still felt good.

————•••⋅⋚⋅•••————

Is Life Supposed to Go Your Way?

The truth is, we are not all winners. Some of us will never win so much as a bingo game, and the way to happiness is surely coming to terms with our limitations while making the most of our natural endowments. Children don't need pep talks about the rewards of success. They'll get that every time they turn on the TV. What they need, rather, is loving assistance in learning how to fail, with grace and profit too. They need to learn that failure is an inevitable part of human life, that every failure is partial only, and that no failure is final. Parents should help children understand that there are times when losing is better than winning (if winning, for example, would have compromised freedom and integrity), and that living well, becoming the best person one can possibly be, is the only success worth thinking about. —Fredelle Maynard[15]

Another clear contributor to our enlarged sense of entitlement and the respectful behavior lacking in many children's character appears to be the disturbing trend among parents to try to smooth life over for their children. These parents want to make everything go their child's way, to keep them happy regardless of what this may take and to avoid conflict at any cost. If a child wants chicken nuggets for dinner again, she gets them, even if this means three different meals for three different children. If a child does not want to go to bed at bedtime, he does not have to. Not only is this a form of overindulgence, which will be discussed shortly, it also teaches children a terribly misguided and inaccurate lesson. This teaches children to *expect* life to go their way. They begin to believe that not only is life going to go their way, it is *supposed* to. Nothing could be further from the truth. What a disabling falsehood this is. What we net is a child who becomes an obnoxious, demanding and spoiled prince or princess. We also end up with children who are handicapped, as in *less able to function.* Heaven forbid that any of these children ever fall seriously ill (they will spend their time bemoaning their illness not fighting it), ever find employment (bosses frequently do not do what you want), ever marry (need I say anything?), or worst of all, ever have children of their own!

We need to teach our children exactly the opposite. We need to teach them the truth: 1)Life is *not* going to go your way, 2)Get over it, and 3)Learn to handle life's disappointments with some grace. I spend a great deal of time in airports and believe me, there are many adults out there in the real world who don't get this yet. They yell and scream at the gate agents who are supposed to stop the thunder and lightning so their flight can leave on time. They are special; they have things to do! Don't we all? All lessons are easier to learn the younger one is, but this is one of the most difficult and costly to learn later in life, especially with regard to physical and emotional health.

Our most gifted, talented, and beautiful children are most at risk for missing this lesson early in their lives. Life does tend to go your way naturally when you have academic and physical gifts. A child with any disability or challenge gets hit early with this important lesson that life is not fair and will not always go your way. He tends to develop some character along with his disability. The first group, the most gifted, may not. A woman in a parenting group burst into tears once as I was suggesting this. She told us that she had been one of the "blessed." She had excelled in elementary and high school, had been chosen as a cheerleader, dated the quarterback, been on homecoming court, gone to the college of her choice, married the man of her dreams, and had three healthy, talented children. At age 37, her husband left her for a younger woman. It was a terrible blow. Anyone in these circumstances would feel betrayed and would suffer, whether they have been taught that life is going to go their way or not. The point here is that those who have recognized that life will not always go their way have a leg up on those who have not; they are less handicapped, if you will. Life will have shown them the ways to begin at the bottom and build again. They will persevere despite a setback. This woman did get through this trial, and she did learn the lesson, but it is a much easier and cheaper lesson at three years old to be told that dinner is going to be spaghetti not chicken nuggets. A temper tantrum is a much smaller price to pay. When our children are told no at a young age, they learn: 1)no means no, 2)grownups *do* need to be listened to, and 3)life will not always go your way. They begin to develop frustration tolerance and the ability to cope successfully with frustration, a very important life skill. Indeed, these children develop some character. There are numerous opportunities for us with our children to teach and model the handling of disappointing, irritating or awkward situations with grace. Sadly for us, the more difficult modeling teaches more than our talking does.

Overindulgence
"There are risks and costs to a program of action. But they are far less than the long range risks and costs of comfortable inaction." —John F. Kennedy

It may seem blunt and nasty, but it has to be said: some of us are wimpy slacker parents. When our children want something from us they whine, cry, complain and gnash their teeth, and because we hate to see them unhappy, we give in. Well, all right, it's not just that we don't want to see them unhappy: we don't have the energy to act. We feel we do not have the energy nor the inclination to discipline right at this moment, after a very long day at work, after a day of dealing with another child's illness, or after worrying about this month's mortgage and car payment. But we have to: it comes with the territory.

Our job as parents is to set loving boundaries and firm rules for our children. We must guide them towards the right choices in life and help them to accept their own limitations and those of the people around them. Our children need to learn to make decisions that, although sometimes uncomfortable, consider the needs of others as well as themselves. Who of you hasn't sat in a restaurant trying to find a moment of calm in an otherwise busy life, only to discover that the parents of small children are allowing them to use the tables and chairs for a boisterous game of tag, or are, at nine o'clock at night, expecting the rest of the room to find the fussing of their nine-month-old endearing? Let us be candid with one another: that baby should have been put to bed a while ago and, even if he can't be, the rest of us shouldn't have a quiet evening disturbed by these inconsiderate parents. Don't get me wrong. I think small children are wonderful and that their games are entertaining and enjoyable, but a public park with trees and swing sets is a more appropriate place to enjoy them. When *we* don't understand courtesy and the rights of others, how will we teach it to our children?

Our children must learn that they have an important role to play in our community and that they must act responsibly and with respect for the needs of others. We must teach them that the choices they make have an impact on their lives and the lives of others, but that the choices they make aren't the only ones that matter in the larger scheme of things. We cannot take the risk that what they are learning from us is that they have a right to please themselves, no matter what. Life isn't just about the pursuit of happiness. If it were, then there is so much that simply wouldn't get done. Who would clean toilets, collect trash, pay bills or even change a baby's diaper? Not everything we do is going to find us immediate happiness, but it still has to be done. How will they hold down a job or follow instructions from an employer if all they know is that they need to be happy? How will they maneuver the trials and tribulations of a good marriage if we have reared them to consider their own needs above all others? And, if their tool chest of negotiating strategies consists of whining, ignoring, getting sick or throwing temper tantrums, what do you think their success rate will be? Are they not truly handicapped? We cannot afford to fail at teaching them that although we value their ideas, thoughts and feelings, we must be the parents and often make the decisions for them, for our family's health, and with consideration for the community at large. We cannot expect to use a fully democratic approach with those not old enough to vote; they simply don't have the developmental (cognitive) or life (experiential) skills to make these important decisions.

When we fail to provide loving structure, guidance and teaching to our children then we have abdicated our roles as parents. If we are going to accept that character is about moral excellence and firmness and a complex of mental and ethical traits, then we cannot afford to over-indulge our children in their every whim and fancy.

The following section is taken from an unpublished document written by Jean Illsley Clarke and used with her permission. For more excellent information on indulgence, please refer to Ms. Clarke's *Growing Up Again: Parenting Ourselves, Parenting Our Children*[16] and *Connections: The Threads That Strengthen Families.*[17]

What is Indulgence?
Indulgence is a form of child neglect. It is giving children too much, too soon, too long. It is giving them things that are not appropriate for their age or their interests and talents. It is giving them things that are really for the parents, not for the children.

What is the Effect of Indulgence on Children?
When Children are Indulged:
❖They think the world owes them.

❖They expect to get what they want because they
    want it.
❖They do not understand delayed gratification and
    therefore are not able to use it when it is
    appropriate.
❖They do not understand what is enough.
❖They expect people to know what they need and to
    take care of them.
❖They lack competencies that other people take for
    granted.

Why Do Parents Indulge and What Can They Do Instead?
❖Parents indulge because they want the child to be
    happy.
Express joy with a child when he is happy and
    comfort him when he is sad.

❖Parents indulge because they want the child to have
    what they didn't have.
Give children what they truly need. Don't give things
    just because you didn't have them.

❖Parents indulge because they were indulged as
    children and that's how they know how to
    parent so they pass the indulgence on.
Learn what experiences children need.
Each stage of development has some tasks children
    need to do for themselves.

❖Parents indulge because they try to buy love.
Love can't be bought. Give unconditional love freely.
Don't get upset when your children say they don't
    like you.

❖Parents indulge because they are afraid of a child's
    anger or disfavor.

Anger is a normal feeling. All children have it.

Teach children to express their anger in appropriate
ways.

Do whatever you need to do to overcome your own
fear of anger or discord.

❖Parents indulge because they give love without
balancing it with appropriate rules, skills and
structures.

Teach skills. Make appropriate rules and carry
through on them.

❖Parents indulge because they give things to ease
their own guilt.

When you feel guilty, change your behavior. Don't try
to ease your guilt by buying things for the
kids.

❖Parents indulge because they project their needs
onto their children so they give children things
that have a price tag. "I never got to go to
hockey camp so you are going to hockey
camp, and you had better be captain of the
team."

Don't expect your children to do what you wanted to
do. Let them develop their own interests and
talents.

❖Parents indulge when they give children things that
are inappropriate because they don't know
child development, the needs and tasks of
each age.

Learn what toys are appropriate for each age.

Remember that ads for toys are written to make
money for toy manufacturers, not to make
good kids.

❖Parents indulge because they do contrary-parenting. They feel rebellious toward the strictness of their own parents and so they swing the pendulum all the way and give everything the children ask for.

Give children everything they need and some of what they want.

❖Parents indulge because they yield to pressure. The pressure of advertising, peers, family or the children themselves.

Make up your own mind about how to raise your children. Don't let peer pressure or kid pressure do your thinking for you.

❖Parents indulge because they are people who are habitually co-dependent, who think and feel for other people, make decisions for them and take care of them without asking them if they want or need the care.

Don't think and feel for children. Teach them to think and feel for themselves.

❖Parents indulge because indulgence is the path of least resistance.

Remember that raising children is the most important job of your life. Give it the energy and education that your most important career deserves. —Jean Illsley Clarke

Good *To* versus Good *For*

Sometimes it is helpful for parents to consider their decisions on whether to give in to a child's demands or wishes by considering the difference between being good *to* or being good *for* a child. Being good to a child can be fun, nice and easy, but when it is in contradiction to being good for the child, it is important to choose good for. If we were always good to a child, we would give him cookies whenever he wanted. But if we are good for the child, he must wait until after dinner. If we are good to her, she may go to bed anytime she feels like it; if we are good for her, she must go to bed at a reasonable bedtime. If you must fight your own personality over this issue, do so—and win. Your child's character depends on your strength. Remember, if you truly love someone, you are willing to put their best interests first. Long term best interest beats short term easy or quick fix anytime. Do not give in when it is wrong to do so. Stand strong, choose one battle or issue at a time and take a stand.

You are not your child's friend. This is not to say that you should not be friendly to your child. Of course, you should, but do not confuse this with being his friend. You are not; you are his parent. Being a mother or father is a far more noble and vital position than being a friend. Your children will have many friends and will change friends during their lifetimes; most likely, they will have but one mother and one father. Why would anyone give this up to be a friend? Why would anyone abdicate this most important of all jobs?

Misunderstanding Self-esteem

There is a misconception that high self-esteem is a good thing no matter what, that it matters not on what it is built. This is untrue. Many children have built their self-esteem in unhealthy ways and on unhelpful foundations which also tend to be extremely shaky. For example, some young children and many adolescent boys feel that much of their value comes from their ability to be aggressive, to win arguments or decisions by force. Many children who become aggressive cannot rely upon academic success or good peer relations to achieve self-esteem and connectedness. Instead, they develop their self-esteem around power and physical superiority. Early experiences as victims, models of aggression in actuality or virtuality, combined with the culture's focus on male strength and superiority all encourage this behavior. Unfortunately, these children require victims to maintain their self-esteem. They must continue behaviors that create trouble for them and those around them. These behaviors are counterproductive to cooperation, kindness, problem solving and just generally getting along. In addition, the self-esteem of aggressive children appears to be vulnerable and fragile.[18]

As discussed earlier, many children are taught they are valuable because they like to watch television or play video games. We give them booklets entitled "All About Me," where they describe "what I like to eat" or "my favorite toy." The problem with this type of activity is that it directs children's attention to their own inner gratification. Lilian Katz in "Self-Esteem and Narcissism: Implications for Practice"[19] states that many practices designed to develop self-esteem may instead be encouraging narcissism.

Empty praise and flattery can help a child believe she has value because she is cute or she can color. Almost all preschoolers can color, and none of them is producing fine art. These pictures are precious art to you because your child made them for you or gave them to you, but they are not high quality art. Let's just tell them the truth. Coloring, when you are a preschooler, is for fun and learning. Their picture has value as a gift, not as fine art.

We have for too long over-praised (in quality and quantity) our young children's productions at a time when they generally put forth little effort and spend most of their time playing and learning (a simultaneous activity). When they get to a certain place in school, elementary school for some, but not until high school or university for others, where they need to put forth real effort, they are often unable to do so. They expect to be praised at the same level that they were when they were younger, while putting forth almost no effort. We have confused and misled them about motivation with our over-abundant praise, and we have decreased not increased their motivation.

What if instead, they had come to accept that they had value because they are alive, from the fact that they exist in our lives, apart from what they do?[20] Self-esteem built on existence is sturdy and foundational, unaffected by the whims of mistakes and failure. It is a strong and healthy belief that we each have much value simply because we exist. Because this type of self-esteem is unshakeable, once built, it allows us to risk all and go for broke, in other words, to be unflinchingly and completely motivated.

And when we must rely upon our accomplishments as a basis for some of our self-worth, why not use virtuous behaviors like persistence, prudence, helpfulness, generosity, or kindness, or the ability to get along with others and maintain harmony? What about focusing on initiative and problem solving and determination? These are much better achievements upon which to build value.

Albert Camus said, "Life is the sum of your choices." While we are discussing self-esteem, let us not overlook teaching children that they are valuable, that they do matter, that their lives are meaningful, and that their choices count. We each get to determine the quality of our lives with our choices of behavior and attitude. What power we hold in our hands, not power over others but power over ourselves. Teach your children it is their responsibility to seize this power and give their lives the meaning they choose. Each of us determines who we are and who we will be. Make certain it is someone you are comfortable with; you can get away from everyone but yourself. It seems we become who we choose to be, step by step. We must be vigilant at each step.

> Watch your thoughts; they become words.
> Watch your words; they become actions.
> Watch your actions; they become habits.
> Watch your habits; they become character.
> Watch your character; it becomes your
> destiny. —Frank Outlaw

As parents, we make a difference in our children's lives. What we say and do count hugely. Scarily. It takes courage to be a parent, especially a good parent. Why didn't someone tell us before we had children?

> No one ever became extremely wicked suddenly. —Juvenal, Roman writer

Accountability and Self-esteem

"To be a man is to be responsible." Antoine de Saint-Exupéry

Teachers from all over the United States and Canada are reporting to me that parents want their help in teaching their children responsibility. We all recognize responsibility as an important component of maturing. However, these same teachers also say that more and more parents are cautioning them not to ever hold their son or daughter accountable for anything that might upset them, cause them pain, or lower their self-esteem. Mary Pipher, in her insightful book, *The Shelter of Each Other: Rebuilding Our Families*[21] says:

> Many clients are more worried about their children's feelings than their behavior and they focus more on their self-esteem than their character. They want their children to be happy more than they want them to be good. It's understandable that parents feel this way, but it's misguided. Happiness ultimately comes from a sense that one is contributing to

the well-being of the community. In reality,
making wise moral choices is the most direct
route to true happiness.

If we consider that self-esteem can be defined as the estimate
of the value we place on ourselves, in other words, how much
we think we are worth, we begin to understand that healthy,
solid self-esteem is liking oneself, being comfortable with
who one is and what one chooses to do; it is having peace and
comfort with regard to oneself. It is high and realistic self-
regard. It is a *result* of good choices, not just a cause or source
of them.

The only way we are going to feel comfortable with
ourselves is if we fairly consistently choose to do the right
thing. When we allow ourselves to do what we know is
wrong, we lose some of our comfort with and respect for
ourselves. In short, our value decreases; our self-esteem is
diminished. If we try to short circuit the process and overlook
what we have done or try not to own wrong choices, they only
get buried deep within ourselves; they do not go away.
Ultimately, they bring us down literally and figuratively.
Thus, holding children (and ourselves) accountable for their
behavior, good and bad, is an essential ingredient in the
establishment of true self-regard. Held accountable, forced to
own *all* of our choices and actions, right and wrong, we tend
to back away more frequently from wrong and choose the
more difficult right. And as a result of these prudent choices,
we get to like ourselves even better in the long term.
Accountability, the ownership of behavior, is an essential
ingredient to high self-esteem and true self-regard.

Separate Deed from Doer?

There seems to be some question as to whether we
own all of our behavior. Many parents question whether
children own all of their behavior. Do we adults own all of
our behavior? Please note that I did not ask whether we are

comfortable owning all of our behavior. The question is simply do we own our behavior? The answer is an unqualified yes. Do children own all of their behavior? The answer again is yes they most certainly do. The confusion seems to center around whether children understand all of their behavior and all of the ramifications. The answer to that is, of course, no they do not. At times, even grownups do not foresee the ramifications and consequences of their behavior. The first grade boy who took a gun to school and shot and killed his classmate did not, I believe, understand what it means to die, let alone to take someone's life. An eighteen year old does, but young children do not yet fully grasp the concept of death; they do not separate real from pretend well. This young boy does, however, own taking the gun to school and the shooting. He knew he was not supposed to take a gun to school. Although I do not expect many first graders to resist such a temptation, he did know. Further, it does not matter whether he knew it was right or not in terms of ownership: he does own the shooting. Who else owns this? His guardians own leaving a loaded gun where a young child could find it, and they own not supervising him and the gun carefully enough. They contributed hugely to this tragedy. But the little boy will, heartbreakingly, own this shooting and killing for the rest of his life. I wish this were not so, but it is. It would be wrong to mislead our children into believing they do not own their behavior. We must not back down from this truth, harsh as it may be. It is a major safeguard against choosing to do wrong and an indispensable ingredient in building good and strong character.

Hopefully we are in agreement that it is essential to hold children (everyone) accountable for *all* of their behavior. This brings us to yet another misconception. The suggestion that we need to separate deed from doer has long been used as a behavior management technique with children. If you do not recognize its name, you may recognize its sound. We were taught never to tell children we don't like them, rather we were to tell them that we don't like what they did, their behavior: "I like you; I don't like your behavior." Although it remains harmful to tell a child we don't like them, the separate deed from doer is at least equally as harmful and wrong on three counts. This technique taught to and used by most educators and many parents is in violation of three important beliefs we each have. It is a threefold violation of our own integrity, our own belief system. Truly, if we want to develop children with integrity, we will need to model it for them and do our level best not to violate our own integrity. Integrity is the quality of being upright and consistent in principle and action; it is the ability to practice what we believe. It is rarely easy and generally quite difficult to manage this when we are dealing with children. Let us now look at the three integrity violations surrounding separate deed from doer.

The first place we run into trouble with our own belief system is with the "I like" and "I don't like" aspect of the technique. Discipline is not about what I like and don't like. That would be about me. Discipline is about the child, the child's needs, best interests, and lessons needed. Sometimes when we discipline, we falter and use our love as a tool, generally to manipulate a child into better behavior. For example, you have a child who never cleans up his messes. And then one day, the miracle takes place: he cleans up all of his room beautifully and thoroughly. You walk in and see this miracle and immediately hug him and tell him you love it (or him) when he cleans up like this.

Another scenario might involve choosing to ignore some usually minor misbehavior by temporarily removing attention, affection, and/or approval. For example, a child fails to pick up his toys properly so we barely talk to him at dinner. When we do either of these, offering affection or approval for behaviors we like or withdrawing them for behaviors we do not, we are in violation of a very important principle, unconditional love. The question to ask ourselves is when are we supposed to love our children? The answer is: *all of the time.* How much of our love—affection, attention and approval are all ways we demonstrate love—is to be available to them at any given time? All of it. If, however, we give extra love (hugs and pats) for cleaning up or behaving positively, or we remove some (withdraw our attention or approval) for undesirable behaviors, we have just changed our love into conditional love. Unconditional love is by far the healthier variety. Remember, we cannot offer both; they are mutually exclusive. Once we have placed one condition on our love, we change it to conditional love. One cannot love 'mostly' unconditionally. It is only unconditional love which is emotionally healthy.

If you are not convinced, consider this scenario from the teen years. Your daughter is in the backseat of a car with her boyfriend. He is telling her that she can be his girlfriend, that he will shower her with attention and affection, he just needs her to change her behavior a little—take off her clothes. Most of us recognize the line, "If you loved me, you would." The concern, of course, is that she has a history of altering her behavior just a bit (putting on shoes, brushing teeth, cleaning her room, working harder on homework) for her parents' and teachers' affection or approval. Although she is not certain that this is the time or the place or the guy or the act, she once again alters her behavior to get what she regards as affection and love, for this is a means she recognizes to obtain love. What we all want in that car is a girl who understands real and healthy love, who tells her boyfriend, "Either you love me or you don't. Which is it? And I will decide what I am doing with my clothes." We also want to rear sons who don't use tricky or manipulative behavior on women and who understand real love as well.

The conclusion we are drawing here is that love needs to be removed from *the act of discipline,* not the concept but the actual disciplining. It is never about whether or not I like it or you when you pick up your toys; discipline is about right and wrong. Discipline is about the fact that, "It is your responsibility to pick up your room." Period. I love you all of the time; bask in its warmth and nurture and be certain of it. It is ever-present and never-changing. The state of your room has nothing to do with whether or not I love you nor how much. Discipline teaches simply, "You need to pick up," or "When you pick up, then you can go on with your life." Discipline is never about whether I love you. I do. You still need to pick up. There is no need to cloud the discipline lesson with the issue of my love. This is an important point.

The second integrity violation is one of honesty. In reality, we have never separated deed from doer. When you meet someone, how do you determine whether you like them or not? By how they act? Their behavior? Of course this is how we decide. No one likes serial killers. Yet most serial killers are quite nurturing and responsive to others. When interviewed by the media after the killer has been arrested, his elderly neighbor always talks about how the just-arrested serial killer/neighbor brought her homemade soup when she was ill and how he carried dog biscuits for all of the neighborhood dogs when he took walks. Serial killers also tend to very closely follow the law. They do not roll through stop signs, nor exceed the speed limit; they cannot afford to draw police attention to themselves. Thus, about 99% of the time, serial killers behave wonderfully, they are nice and good. For that one, isolated behavior (killing) that takes up less than 1% of their actual lifetimes, would you consider inviting these people to dinner? The answer is no, of course not. We do not like them nor want them around—simply and only because they kill. Killing is a behavior. We do not separate deed from doer. Indeed, later we will discuss the need to teach children that *they are what they do* in order to build good character. Thus, trying to tell a child that we like him and not his behavior is tantamount to lying to him. It simply is not true. The real issue is not whether or not we like the behavior; the real issue is that the behavior is wrong.

Lastly, separating deed from doer is an accountability transgression. Discipline must always include accountability, ownership of behavior. That is to say, discipline always includes the lesson, "You are responsible for what you do and for what happens to you and others as a result of your actions." Stated simply, we own every single thing we do and the consequences. One can't get much farther from ownership of behavior than separating deed from doer. When one is separate from his behavior, it is no longer a part of him, and he does not have to own it. This is wrong. It is no wonder that we have confused our children. On the one hand, we tell them they must be responsible and accountable for what they choose to do, that they own their behavior. Then we use a technique like separate deed from doer and send them the opposite message. Generally, when we violate our own integrity and put into practice, knowingly or unknowingly, some principle we do not believe in, we send a conflicted and confusing message that breaks down emotional health rather than builds it. As well, we model incongruity, not integrity.

Once again, it is not harmful for a child to own all behavior, even misbehavior. When misbehavior occurs, and it will, our job is to discipline the offender. For example, if a sibling hits her sister, try telling her, "You do not have the right to hurt anyone—ever." We can also separate the aggressive sibling from her sister teaching the lesson that if you abuse the privilege of being with your sister, you lose it for a time. Follow up with problem solving and teaching how to handle this problematic situation with a sister. If the sister called a brother stupid, teach him to remember or discover that this is untrue and to disregard it. If one sister is not pulling her weight picking up a shared room, set up a schedule. There are many ways to solve any problem without the use of aggression and violence. One must first own the misbehavior in order to learn from it. Discipline means to teach; misbehavior tells us what to teach. Learning is enhanced and enabled by ownership.

The music thumped deep in her chest as she swayed to its rhythm. Jenna was certain she had never felt so alive. Her hair brushed against her shoulders as she moved and she was pleasantly warm from the activity. Dancing always made her feel more connected to something bigger and less controlled in her life. She could forget the failures, mistakes and heartaches of the week in the fatigue brought on by movement. It was almost the only time she felt happy. Dancing, dancing, dancing, and of course, a few drinks to make her feel less inhibited.

As the evening wore on she felt more and more hazy, her vision spirited away by the energy of the dance and the effects of the alcohol. The music sounded better, if a little distant, as the evening wore on. She smiled and laughed, feeling omnipotent and beautiful. Aware that her dancing partner was speaking to her, she turned seeking the source of his voice. He seemed to be tall, with dark closely cropped hair. His shirt was blue, his pants khaki. He spoke suddenly from behind her shoulder, his arm reaching around to hold her upright in the middle.

Jenna tried to focus on what he was saying. "Let's go up to my room. You look like you need to sit down," he said, and snuggled in a tickley way into her neck, his tongue brushing lightly by her ear. He smelled like beer, yes, but awfully good. "Come on, follow me," he said, taking her by the hand. Lightheaded, and awkward suddenly on her feet, Jenna stumbled behind him. The climb up the stairs was not as easy as it should have been. The fraternity was packed tonight, people milling about in the hallways and in and out of all the rooms. The lineup outside the bathroom was long and the noise of many people talking made conversation impossible. When they arrived at the boy's room, Jenna was relieved to be out of the commotion of the hallways. She slumped down onto the bed, giddy with drink and the evening's activity.

Jenna tried to look around the room, to make sense of where she really was. The guy, she could see, was busy throwing clothing from the floor into the closet and then sitting at the computer and getting music ready on the MP3 player. He seemed far away, and she realized suddenly that she didn't know his name. When he came to join her on the bed, he moved slowly in and out of her vision. His voice, low and insistent, said: "I think you should stay here. Let me help you get your jeans off."

"No. No, it's okay," she said. "I should probably go home now."

"But you don't have to. You can stay right here. I'll take care of you." Moving his hands to her waist, he said again, "Let me help you take those off." He leaned in close to her face, smiling. He did smell awfully good and his hands, massaging her stomach, very good. When he leaned forward to kiss her, Jenna was overcome by how natural it seemed. He smelled so good; his kiss was soft and comforting. How could she go home now? In her foggy state, lethargy seemed a rational solution...and a fun one at that. Jenna was there for the night.

Next morning, vomiting into the toilet down the hall, she was horrified. She could hear the guys out in the hall, laughing about Doug's success the night before. Washing her face at the sink, looking into her own puffy eyes and at her pallid skin, she felt ashamed and dirty. What had felt wonderful and spontaneous just hours before seemed cheap and unpleasant now. How would she face this guy? What would she tell her roommates? What had she been thinking? She wanted to die, to vanish, and to slip through the linoleum floor of the bathroom into some alternate universe. With her back to the closed door, she slipped down the door until she was seated on the floor. Pulling her knees in close to her chest, she began to cry. First, there was a rivulet of tears, next painful racking sobs.

Now, it is easy for us as parents reading this to say that this awful boy took advantage of this poor girl. There is no argument here; this young man took advantage of her vulnerability. However, who is and always will be responsible for this young woman's moral well-being? She is. Our children need to learn early in their lives that they are responsible for their own actions, and their own results, and that if they do not look to protecting their own moral well-being, they can't be certain that others will. I might say that this is true of the young man in this story as well. He had a responsibility to himself and his own moral integrity. How is it that a young man this age doesn't know that he has unfairly taken advantage of another person? How is it that he doesn't care what this might mean to another, vulnerable person? He is guilty of having cared very little for his own moral integrity and for having treated another human being, who needed his support, with disrespect. Don't get me wrong here. Finding another person attractive, appealing and comforting is not usually considered wrong. We, as human beings, have a variety of emotional and sexual needs. What seemed to go wrong here is that these young people did not make their choices with sound minds or with clear thinking about their actions and their potential consequences or outcomes.

I remember having a conversation with my then sixteen-year-old daughter about the dangers of alcohol. We were driving to a basketball practice (never underestimate what you will learn being the driver of a bunch of kids to their activities) and she asked me why, if alcohol were prohibited, did so many people seek it out and consider those who drank the life of the party? A few minutes contemplation brought me to a difficult decision. I needed to tell her the truth. People drink because it makes them feel good, because they find it easier to be social, and because sometimes it makes them more fun-loving. In short, I told her, alcohol can soothe your inhibitions and enable you to behave in ways you wouldn't ordinarily if you were sober. Your inhibitions are there because they are an expression of who you are and what you are comfortable with. Some of our inhibitions may not be entirely healthy, and they may need to be addressed at some point in our lives, but some of them are just there because that is who we are. That means, then, that you need to consider carefully under what circumstances you wish to decide not to be who you are, or to try on another type of behavior. My daughter, often wise beyond her years, agreed. She had noticed that many of her friends' experimentation had led to embarrassment and public disgrace. The same friends who urged you on often didn't support you later. I shared some stories and observations from my university years that mirrored her own impressions. It was an important opportunity for us to share our thoughts about appropriate behavior and doing the right thing with respect to our own moral well-being.

It is clear then that we must rethink much of what we have been taught to do with our children. Misconceptions, or violations of integrity are everywhere; the only way through or out of them, is to think our way out: listen to our little voices, who repeat to us our own principles. It is indeed time to get it right with children. First, we will have to get it right with ourselves. Not only must we practice what we believe, we must also teach only that which we believe. Fortunately, our children are worth the effort.

Chapter Checkpoints

✔ Teach children that they are unique, incredibly valuable and precious, but not special. Special connotes and leads to a sense of entitlement, a belief that one is above others and perhaps beyond the law.

✔ Teach children 'no means no' and to develop frustration tolerance through these three most helpful lessons:
>   1. Life is not always going to go your way.
>   2. Get over it.
>   3. Learn to handle disappointments with grace.

✔ An overindulged child is a handicapped child.

✔ Being good *for* a child is more important than being good *to* him.

✔ Self-esteem needs not just to be built; it must be built on sound principles. We must teach children that their lives and choices do matter. It is their job to give their lives the meaning that they choose. Positive self-regard is the result of good choices.

✔ Like it or not, we own all of our behavior. This accountability is a safeguard against choosing to do wrong and an indispensable ingredient in building good character.

✔ We are what we do.

✔ Life is the sum of our choices. So, too, is our character. It is prudent to make behavioral choices that match our beliefs—integrity is the outcome.

Chapter Five:
Encouraging Character to Grow

Deb's Pappy kept his loose change arranged in piles; dimes, nickels and quarters were all stacked in columns of ascending size in the ancient curio cabinet in the large dining room. Anna had no idea when he built these little towers. In her observation he was always sitting in a large burgundy velour chair sleeping, rather noisily, with the television watching over him. He was, she believed, a kind and generous man. At least she'd never observed any behavior that would indicate otherwise. He paid for her friend Deb's dance lessons and helped to keep their sometimes-troubled family afloat, both financially and spiritually.

And yet, those columns of cold hard cash called. These little girls had needs, for bubble gum, for fruit sours, for boxes of hot french fried potatoes. Surely he wouldn't notice if just a few coins were missing. Stealthily, they had, on numerous occasions, helped themselves to Pappy's largesse. They spirited away the coins and themselves to the nearest convenience store and bought themselves what they could not otherwise have afforded. Hiking home, they stopped in a nearby park to consume their goodies. The sours turned the insides of their cheeks raw and their stomachs nauseous. The licorice blackened their teeth and the packets of bubble gum made their behavior unacceptable to most polite company, but they were content, happy even. Pappy hadn't even noticed.

One Saturday afternoon, however, they returned to Deb's home to find the house in an uproar. Deb's Pappy had died in his sleep that afternoon. The girls, seeking solace from the confusion of the house, sat in the backyard under a large and messy lilac bush. A shiver of disbelief and regret shadowed them to their sheltered spot. Now Anna felt bad. Pappy's gum and sweets felt extremely heavy in her stomach, their weight keeping her rooted to the damp grassy carpet beneath her. Perhaps Pappy had noticed. Perhaps his loss had distressed him so much he had died in a fit of anger. Perhaps he had died of disappointment that these two, to whom he had been so kind, had betrayed his trust. Perhaps it was just that his columns had gotten shorter. It was hard for girls of nine to know how death had come about.

Some years later, Deb would move from that house to one much closer in to town, but not before Anna had made her peace. One quiet winter afternoon, while Deb was collecting her jacket and gloves, she had returned to the curio cabinet with coins saved up for just such an opportunity and placed a tower of quarters next to a china salt and pepper shaker. It was not quite as tidy as Pappy's shaky hands had built, but it was a tower to be proud of nonetheless.

Act Right, Feel Right
"Art, like morality, consists of drawing the line somewhere."
—G.K. Chesterton

"The measure of a man's character is what he would do if he knew he never would be found out." —Baron Thomas Babington Macauley

In Chapter Four, we discussed the importance of accountability in building positive self-regard. One of the most fundamental and important precepts we can teach our children is: act right, feel right; act wrong, feel wrong. In the late 1960s, we took feeling good to new heights and many of my generation made feeling good the goal of their lives. With regard to developing character, this is a misguided and mistaken goal. This is not to suggest that feeling good is not fun, appropriate at times, and makes life feel worth living. However, feeling good caused by bad choices and poor behavior does not contribute to character nor to true positive self-regard. Feeling good must not come at the expense of the real objective: feeling right. This is one of the principles we need to teach—one of the lines we need to draw.

The goal for ourselves and for our children is to feel *right*. When we feel right about ourselves, we move toward tranquility, contentment with ourselves, and true positive self-regard. Let us look at a concrete example. If a student decides not to do his homework but rather to play video games, watch television, and play with his friends instead, he will feel just fine, feel good even, while he continues on this path. However, when his report card arrives, things may change. His grades will quite likely suffer. If his parents are wise enough not to tell him how awful he should feel, he will feel bad, whether he admits this or not. No one feels right about a poor performance, especially when one knows he did not put forth effort. What we have is a child who chose to act wrong (not to do schoolwork) and *as a result,* feels wrong. If he wishes to feel better about himself, to feel right, he will need to choose to act right, to do the required schoolwork. When we act right, we feel right, and when we act wrong, we feel wrong. This is as it is supposed to be.

Emotional Pain
"The gem cannot be polished without friction." —Proverb

"Character cannot be developed in ease and quiet. Only through experience of trial and suffering can the soul be strengthened, vision cleared, ambition inspired, and success achieved." —Helen Keller

Lessons learned in pain usually last forever.

Let us talk about feeling wrong. Feeling wrong can be upsetting; it can even be painful. Do we want our children in emotional pain? Think about this: it is a very important question. Wanting to keep our children from pain is a normal and natural aspiration for a parent. Yet, it is truly impossible and at times quite unhelpful. The fact is we want and need our children to be in emotional pain on occasion. Let me be very clear. It is not beneficial for us to hurt our children, to cause our children pain of any sort; this is not what is being suggested. What is being referred to is the pain a child causes *himself* with poor behavioral decisions. What is being suggested is that at times our children are going to choose to act wrong—they are after all children whose job description includes misbehaving and making poor decisions. Another way to phrase this is that children have so much to learn. Some of this learning may be accompanied by pain. When misbehavior takes place, we must not too quickly soothe them nor console them in ways that take away from or extinguish the lesson's impact.

Trick Thinking

A mother approached me about too quick soothing and inappropriate consoling of her eighteen year old son. She had left her son alone for three days and nights shortly after he had graduated from high school. He had two responsibilities: to go to work and to water and feed their family dog who resided on their back porch. When this mother returned, sadly, she found the dog dead and the water dish empty. Summer heat and thirst are not a good mix in Texas. When her son returned from work, he was devastated. He loved this dog who had been his companion for 16 years. He felt so awful that his mother immediately began to console him. She said, "You didn't mean to let him die." It doesn't matter; the dog is still dead. (Drunk drivers always say they didn't mean to kill your family. Well, they needed to mean *not to*: they needed to mean never to get into a car after drinking.) She also told him, "He was an old dog; we knew he wouldn't make it to the new year." Is it better to let an old dog die than a puppy? Is it alright not to take care of the elderly and infirm? These are rationalizations or trick thinking. They are also wrong. I would console this child with a hug and words to the effect: "I bet you wish you hadn't done this" or "I bet you wish you could change this." Both of these would be true; neither is a trick thinking form of rationalization. It seems many in our population have learned not only to rationalize their behavior but also that this rationalization somehow excuses and erases wrong behavior. This is not true.

The Lessons of the Tunnels

We also want this young man to be in pain over this for two very important reasons. First, each of us wants our own children to experience real emotional pain while they are still living with us and under our supervision. We need them to learn the three lessons of the tunnels.[22]

> 1. **Expect tunnels in your life.** Everyone's life will contain problems: "misfortune comes to all men." Coming to terms with this fact allows us to avoid becoming too terribly upset when we do face adversity or loss. These are parts of life, every life. Acknowledging this allows us to accept the reality of problems and lets us move towards solving them.

> 2. **Tunnels can be navigated.** Problems can be solved. We will need bright, functioning

headlights and excellent driving skills, and sometimes outside help, but we can navigate the dark times.

3. There is light at the end of every tunnel.
Don't give up hope. Pain eases and life goes on. We can endure suffering and we can come out stronger and better for it.

We need our children to learn and to believe in these lessons before they leave us. They can be tremendous buffers against discouragement, despair, and even suicide.

Secondly, if we allow the above teen to experience this pain, and it will be a great deal of pain, since the dog was beloved by him, this is the first adolescent I would ask to watch my own dog. The reason is that he has not only learned his lesson about caring for pets, he has learned it in pain. Lessons learned in pain stick. I know that this young man would leave a party to go feed and water a dog. He knows a pet can die without care; he is a believer.

Let us consider what this young man developed during this experience. He developed character and conscience. Both are qualities we desire. Think back to any situation or experience when you were actively building character. Was it not accompanied by pain? Whenever I ask groups of adults this question, everyone agrees that during the times they were building character and conscience, they experienced pain. The conclusion is that if we deny children pain, specifically the pain they cause themselves, we effectively deny them the opportunity to build character and conscience. We do indeed want and need our children in emotional pain on occasion. I am not asking you to enjoy this pain; that would be sadistic and unhealthy. Yet some of the most important parenting that I have done has been watching and holding a child in pain and biting my tongue—allowing the pain to exist. I have yet to ever find this easy or comfortable. It is, however, in my children's best interest.

Inez confided in her father about her feelings about life and how things were so hard for her. She did not know how she was going to make it and she wanted to give up. She was tired of fighting and struggling. It seemed that just as one problem was solved another arose. Inez was twelve; most twelve-year-olds' lives are troublesome to them.

Her father, a chef, took her to the kitchen, filled three pots with water and placed the fire on high. Soon the three pots came to a boil. In one he placed carrots, in the other he placed eggs, and in the last he placed ground coffee beans. He let them sit and boil, without saying a word.

The daughter sucked her teeth, impatiently wondering what he was trying to do. She had problems, and he was making this strange concoction. In half an hour he walked over to the stove and turned down the fire. He pulled the carrots out, drained them and placed them in the bowl. He lifted the eggs out and placed them in another bowl. Then he ladled the coffee out and placed it in a third. Turning to her he asked, "Darling, what do you see?"

With a fair bit of impatience, she replied, "Carrots, eggs, and coffee."

Taking her arm, he brought her closer and asked her to feel the carrots. She did and noted that they were soft. He then asked her to take an egg and break it. After pulling off the shell, she observed that the egg was hard-boiled. Finally, he asked her to sip the coffee. Her face frowned from the strength of the coffee. Humbly, she asked, "What does it mean, Father?"

He explained. "Each of these things faced the same adversity, 212 degrees of boiling water. Each, however, reacted differently. The carrot went in strong, hard, and unrelenting, but after going through boiling water, it softened and became weak. The egg was fragile, a thin outer shell protecting a liquid center. After sitting through the boiling water, its inside became hardened. The coffee beans are unique. After they were in the boiling water, they became stronger and richer." He paused, then asked, "Which are you?"

When adversity knocks on your door, how do you respond? Are you a carrot, an egg, or a coffee bean? Are you the carrot that seems hard, but with the smallest amount of pain, adversity or heat, you wilt and become soft with no strength? Are you the egg, which starts off with a malleable heart, a fluid spirit, but after a death, a breakup, a divorce or a layoff, you became hardened and stiff. Your shell looks the same, but you have become bitter and tough.

Or are you like the coffee bean? The bean does not get its peak and robust flavor until it reaches 212 degrees Fahrenheit. When the water gets the hottest, its flavor matures. When things are at their worst, you get better.[23]

————••⋅••————

You Are What You Do
"How many times do you get to lie before you are a liar?"
—Michael Josephson

I was privileged to work with a wonderful Catholic school in Ohio. One of my assignments was to work with the fourth, fifth, and sixth graders, a delightful and open group of students. Since this age of child has been known to toy with us adults, it was great fun to toy with them. I asked them some "what would you do if" questions. For example, what would you do if after playing at your friend's house, you accidentally nicked his mother's car with your bike? You know for certain no one saw you do this. Well, the fourth graders gave us chapter and verse explanations of right from wrong. They would tell the car owner what had happened—no question. Their teachers were quite relieved; the students had clearly been taught well. Then we talked with the fifth and sixth graders, who, by the way, had been taught by these same teachers. They were far more interesting. Developmentally, they were pulling away from the childhood in which the fourth graders still resided. Fifth and sixth graders are beginning to separate from their parents and teachers; they are beginning to find their own identities. They are also developing higher order thinking and more sophisticated reasoning power. They are beginning to rethink and reform their ideas and values in order to internalize them and to make them their own. They are beginning to think for themselves. Sometimes we call this rebellion. Sometimes we label it the developmental stage it is: separation and identification. Adolescents have always done this. It is a developmental task they begin as toddlers and revisit as preteens and generally do not finish until their 20s. It is beautiful to behold and difficult to live with.

The older students asked questions before forming an answer. They asked, "Is it a new car like a Mercedes or just an old Honda?" Do you hear trick thinking? Should what you decide to do be dependent upon the value of the car? They also asked, "Are you sure no one saw?" Many adults still struggle with this one. I am afraid that not only do we seem to have a proclivity toward this type of thinking, parents have unwittingly taught it in an effort to minimize suffering and pain. The fourth graders all said they would tell their friend's mother. I marveled at their courage and wondered how many would actually be able to knock on the door. The older students debated and got slippery on this one. Having taught these students much better behavior, their teachers were surprised and appalled. This age is a great time for teaching.

It was the next question that was most intriguing and revealing. I asked, "What would you do if you had just bought a new computer but had no money left for games, and your friend offers to copy his games for you?" The fourth graders said they would wait. I marveled at their ability to delay gratification and wondered how long they really would wait. More worldly and sophisticated, the fifth and sixth graders immediately said that this was called pirating software. I did not bother to point out that pirates were thieves and that this was a word with a negative origin. Another enjoined with the fact that pirating software is not illegal unless you sell it. We paused here while this author explained copyright law. Yes, it is illegal; it is a form of stealing. Whenever one copies software (CDs, videotapes, etc.), the people who created, produced, or distributed it are cheated out of their share of the income from that sale. Selling it simply breaks a second law. Another student asked whether it was a small or a large software company. His theory was that it's better to steal from a large company with greater profits than to steal from a smaller one with smaller profits. This smacks of trick thinking to me. Naturally, the discussion soon came to whether they would get caught. They agreed that they would not. This conclusion, however, begs the question, even if you aren't caught, aren't you still responsible for having stolen something? This is an important question, one which these kids needed to be challenged by.

In the end, after they had debated back and forth, I had them vote. "How many of you will accept your friend's copied software?" About half said they would not take the pirated software; the other half said they would take it in a heartbeat. In fact, it seemed a little stupid to this group not to accept this gift. Their teachers were again appalled. I simply asked them one more question. "How many of you want to be a thief?" No one raised a hand. One boy, a very bright and articulate lad, turned to me and said, "Ooh, that paints it so differently." I knew that at least one student had gotten it. The point here is that some of these kids wanted to steal, but they did not want to be thieves. As parents and educators, we have failed to teach them that this is impossible. We have failed to teach them that *you are what you do.* Again a caution: I am not suggesting that we go back to name-calling and labeling. These tactics have never been helpful and can be quite harmful. I am suggesting that we teach a simple concept: you are what you do. In fact, we need to teach definitions. If you lie, you are a liar. If you steal, you are a thief.

Most of us on occasion want to *act* like a jerk. We don't want to let someone into a line of traffic, we want to speak disrespectfully or disparagingly to someone who is irritating us, we want more than our share of the juicy, ripe strawberries. What we don't want is to *be* a jerk. We want to lie, just a little, but still be considered honest people, not liars. This simply cannot be so. If you do it, you are it. This is a hard truth.

The next time one of your children hurts a sibling, do not ask the first child if he wanted to hurt his sister—he most likely did. This is the "do" part. Instead, ask him about the "be" part. "Do you want to be a hurtful person? Do you want to be a mean person?" Our children do not want to be cruel and hurtful people if we have taught them our values of good and bad and right and wrong. They do, however, want to hurt on occasion. We must teach them that they can't have it both ways. If you do it, you are it.

Teach Your Values

"The question for the child is not 'Do I want to be good?' But 'Whom do I want to be like?'" —Bruno Bettelheim

"If we are forced, at every hour, to watch or listen to horrible events, this constant stream of ghastly impressions will deprive even the most delicate among us of all respect for humanity." —Cicero (Marcus Tullius), Roman orator

At the Fourth Annual Character Counts! Coalition Meeting, NEA (National Education Association) President Bob Chase reported that Amitai Etzioni, a sociologist estimated that "about half the families no longer see it as their duty to pass along values from generation to generation."[24] This is astonishing. Family values are too important to overlook. We must take the time to teach them. We teach them in two ways, with our words and with our actions, keeping in mind that our verbal lessons are only important to the degree that they agree with our behavior.

It is, of course, imperative that we treat our children with dignity and respect—all of the time. If we are to hear their views and thoughts, we will have to treat these with respect. We will have to treat other people's views with respect as well. There is no quicker way to close up our children than to tell them their idea or point of view is stupid, naive, invalid or unworthy of consideration. Dismissing their ideas is not only callous and unkind, it lacks empathy and connection. It also teaches them that their ideas are not valuable and that is just not so. If we are foolish enough to disparage someone else's opinion, we teach them that it is not safe to disagree with us. Many will close up like clams. They will stop sharing with us.

Teachable Moments

First, be aware of situations that represent

opportunities for ethical or character-developing decisions. Cutting in line is an ethical decision, so is hanging up on someone. Driving offers a host of opportunities for decision making. We make ethical decisions every day all day long: begin to take note of them. They are easy to miss. Talk about the decisions you make and why you believe them to be right and important. Encourage your children to come to you when a decision is difficult; help walk them through various scenarios and their outcomes. The outcome portion is quite important. Do not overlook it. Be aware of when you model wrong behavior. Don't try to rationalize or trick think it away.

Whether your children have made ethical or unethical decisions, take time to talk to them about these decisions. Ask them first how they feel about their choice and their behavior. Are they proud of it? Would they rather others did not know about it? Do they wish they could change it? Hearing about how they arrived at their decision is an important early step in understanding where assistance is needed. Let them talk first.

It is also helpful to review our own behavior with a clear eye. How do we behave? How good is the character we model? Sometimes these incidents come in quick bursts—we let someone have the parking space, we return wrongly counted change, we hold our anger. Other times, we don't demonstrate persistence and fortitude or a consistent belief over time. Either way, we teach.

The pickle jar as far back as I can remember sat on the floor beside the dresser in my parents' bedroom. When he got ready for bed, Dad would empty his pockets and toss his coins into the jar. As a small boy, I was always fascinated at the sounds the coins made as they were dropped into the jar. They landed with a merry jingle when the jar was almost empty. Then the tones gradually muted to a dull thud as the jar was filled. I used to squat on the floor in front of the jar and admire the copper and silver circles that glinted and shone like a pirate's treasure when the sun poured through the bedroom window.

When the jar was filled, Dad would sit at the kitchen table and roll the coins before taking them to the bank. Taking the coins to the bank was always a big production. Stacked neatly in a small cardboard box, the coins were placed between Dad and me on the seat of his old truck. Every time, as we drove to the bank, Dad would look at me hopefully. "Those coins are going to keep you out of the textile mill, son. You're going to do better than me. This old mill town's not going to hold you back, son."

Also, each and every time, as he slid the box of rolled coins across the counter at the bank toward the cashier, he would grin proudly. "These are for my son's college fund. He'll never work at the mill all of his life like me."

We would always celebrate each deposit by stopping for an ice cream cone. I always got chocolate. Dad always got vanilla. When the clerk at the ice cream parlor handed Dad his change, he would show me the few coins nestled in his palm. "When we get home, we'll start filling the jar again." He always let me drop the first coins into the empty jar. As they rattled around with a brief, happy jingle, we grinned at each other. "You'll get to college on pennies, nickels, dimes and quarters," he said. "But you'll get there. I'll see to that." The years passed, and I finished college and took a job in another town. Once, while visiting my parents, I used the phone in their bedroom and noticed that the pickle jar was gone.

It had served its purpose and had been removed. A lump rose in my throat as I stared at the spot beside the dresser where the jar had always stood. My dad was a man of few words and never lectured me on the values of determination, perseverance, and faith. The pickle jar had taught me all these virtues far more eloquently than the most flowery of words could have done.

When I married, I told my wife Susan about the significant part the lowly pickle jar had played in my life as a boy. In my mind, it defined, more than anything else, how much my dad had loved me. No matter how rough things got at home, Dad continued to doggedly drop his coins into the jar. Even the summer when Dad got laid off from the mill and Mama had to serve dried beans several times a week, not a single dime was taken from the jar. To the contrary, as Dad looked across the table at me, pouring catsup over my beans to make them more palatable, he became more determined than ever to make a way out for me. "When you finish college, son," he told me, his eyes glistening, "you'll never have to eat beans again—unless you want to."

The first Christmas after our daughter Jessica was born, we spent the holiday with my parents. After dinner, Mom and Dad sat next to each other on the sofa, taking turns cuddling their first grandchild. Jessica began to whimper softly, and Susan took her from Dad's arms. "She probably needs to be changed," she said, carrying the baby into my parents' bedroom to diaper her. When Susan came back into the living room, there was a strange mist in her eyes. She handed Jessica to Dad before taking my hand and leading me into the room.

"Look," she said softly, her eyes directing me to a spot on the floor beside the dresser. To my amazement, there, as if it had never been removed, stood the old pickle jar, the bottom already covered with coins. I walked over to the pickle jar, dug down into my pocket, and pulled out a fistful of coins. With a gamut of emotions choking me, I dropped the coins into the jar. I looked up and saw that Dad, carrying Jessica, had slipped quietly into the room. Our eyes locked, and I knew he was feeling the same emotions I felt. Neither one of us could speak. We didn't need to speak.[25]

Mistakes: The Best Lessons

Admit your own mistakes. Don't flog yourself over them; use them. Admit them to your children. Mistakes are such glorious opportunities to learn. Mistakes tell us exactly what we are missing and in what areas we are weak. As we learn, we can also teach our children to have the courage to admit and face their mistakes, to have the wherewithal to address, correct or reduce their fallout, and to have the foresight to prevent them from taking place again. Avoid falling into the trap of defending your mistakes; model humility. Show your children that you take the time to examine your own behavior both before and after it takes place. Teach them that examining it prior to its taking place is generally far less painful.

Develop a Moral Compass

Looking closely at their decisions and choices is one method of helping children begin to develop conscience. Often children act and then never think about what has taken place again. Teach your young children to ask themselves this question when they are deciding what to do: Is this something you would want to tell your mother or father? If you would be uncomfortable telling your parents, it's quite likely a wrong choice. If former President Clinton had asked himself whether he would be comfortable telling his wife or his daughter what he was about to do with Ms. Lewinsky, he might have changed the course of history and made his own life much easier and better. Questioning ourselves can be an excellent moral compass.

As children age, the question becomes, "When this moment is over and I'm looking back on it in the future, will I be proud of the person I was and what I did?"[26] Another set of helpful questions is: "What would the world be like if everyone acted the way I do?"[27] Would this be alright if the situation were reversed? What would you want done if you were the other person in the scenario? Answering these questions honestly can help in making the right decision.

Chapter Checkpoints

✔ Act right, feel right. Act wrong, feel wrong. Feeling right outweighs feeling wrong; it also overrules feeling good.

✔ Deny a child the emotional pain he causes himself with his wrong behavior and you effectively deny him the opportunity to build both conscience and character. Character building sessions seem always to be accompanied by pain. Do not be too quick to console; lessons learned in pain tend to stick.

✔ Do not encourage rationalizations and "trick thinking."

✔ Teach "you are what you do." If you are not comfortable being a liar, then don't lie.

✔ Teach your values. Use life situations and decisions. Mistakes, our own especially, are excellent teaching tools.

✔ Teach your children to develop a moral compass, ways to tell whether actions are right or wrong. Helpful questions include:
   "Would I be comfortable telling my mom or dad what I did?"
   "Would this be alright if the situation were reversed?"

Chapter Six:
The Media and Our Children

This evening Marla had arrived home from work with time to prepare a complete meal. John also had arrived home early enough to contribute to the dinner preparations. The kids, one engaged in phone gossip, another flipping channels on the television, and still another outside banging a ball against the wall of the house, seemed oblivious to the efforts on their behalf. When John called to them to come and set the table, there was a not unexpected litany of complaint.

From Tanya: "I'm on the phone. Geez...I'm busy," her eyes rolling for emphasis.

From Sarah: "Why is it always me who has to help? Nobody else ever does anything. Tanya is such a baby. She should get off the phone and help."

Out in the yard, Tucker was oblivious or deaf, an ailment which had recently been selectively afflicting him. He continued to bang his ball against the house. He did not intend to put in an immediate appearance.

"Sarah," John said smiling, "just get started. I'll be the parent and decide who will do what. Thank you. Knives and forks are on the counter." Turning to Tanya, he said firmly, "Tanya. Now is when your help is required. You may speak to your friend again after dinner." Going to the door, he bellowed, "Tucker! Come in now please; you need to help with dinner." Grudgingly, all three were soon grabbing, pushing and grumbling around the table.

Tanya complained that Tucker was stupid and too young to know which sides of the plates the forks and knives went, and Sarah had avoided many to and fros by fussing unnecessarily with the paper napkins, folding them into a flowery design. The table, however, was ready finally and Marla and John carried the hot plates of chicken and rice and gravy to the table. The day was drawing to a close and they were all together again.

Glancing over at Tucker while she served the rice, Marla noticed a nasty bruise and scrape on his left arm, just above his elbow. "How did you get that?" she asked. Tucker, playing dumb again, said nothing. "Tucker," she repeated, "I asked you a question." Still he had no voice, but his shoulders raised and fell in a shrug.

"Those boys from Macon Drive picked on him at recess today," said Sarah. "I thought he should tell the teacher, but he doesn't listen to me." Tucker scowled.

"Is this true, Tucker?" Marla enquired. His body remained closed, except for the nasty welt on his arm. "Honey, I think you could tell us what happened." Jumping up from his chair, Tucker shouted, "I'm fine. Just leave me alone. I don't need to tell anybody. I can take care of myself!" His face grew red with indignation and his sister looked quickly away.

"Alright, alright son," said John. "Perhaps if you are unwilling to tell us, your sisters could just let us know what happened. We're not saying you can't take care of yourself. We just want to know if we can find out what the problem is and what we can think of that will help." Bit by bit the truth came out; Tucker's eyes began to well up and his chin dimpled and trembled. It seemed there were bullies in charge of the school playground, bullies too big for Tucker to manage on his own.

Trying to be helpful, Tanya said, "Oh Tucker, you aren't the only one who is having trouble. We all are. But you got hurt, and they don't have the right to hurt you or anybody." Sarah, putting her arm comfortingly around her little brother, said: "Let Mom and Dad help. I think this is a problem for big people. But don't worry, Tanya and I will stick right by you, okay?"

John and Marla noted with pleasure that her reassurance seemed to relieve Tucker's anxiety. Inwardly, however, they grinned at the irony of the hard-hitting older sister saying no one had the right to hurt him. No one but her, they figured.

Now, it was time to think of strategies and solutions. Just another ordinary dinner.

When we do not find the time to sit and get to know our children, their thoughts, their friends, even just their musical tastes, we leave them vulnerable to the world outside our house. And don't forget: these days, through the television, radio, and Internet, the world marches confidently, and without opposition, right into our houses. If we are not sitting and challenging public opinion and values or asking our children to consider the ethics of any particular decision, someone else, or, more importantly, some marketing agent will tell them what to think and feel. This is a scary thought, don't you think?

Stories: Books and Film

Use books, videos and television programs to discuss the values of right and wrong behavior. The heros and heroines of stories generally tend to set good examples or to have to live with the consequences of poor choices. Don't just read these stories: discuss them. Discuss the characters' choices, whether they were good or bad, what might have happened had a different decision been made. Discuss who was prudent and who was unwise. I am clearly biased in favor of books.[28] Too many films and television programs simply pit good against evil, and offer little portrayal of problem solving, getting along, and compromise. Characters appear, unlike in real life, as all bad or all good; there is no shading, no gray area. Stories and books, however, offer so many other alternatives. When my son, Tim, was in early elementary school, he loved knights and dragons. I tired of the eternal battle between these two foes; on film they always fought, and good always prevailed. When I described Tim's interest and my hesitation to a children's literature specialist, she immediately pulled out two books for me to peruse. The one I chose had a knight and dragon, both hesitant to fight and do battle, decide to open a barbecue place where the knight's armor became the grill and the dragon's fire cooked the hamburgers. Here were problem solving, conflict resolution, and friendship made, not destroyed. There was no good versus evil. Read to your children every night. Find great literature; there are plenty of great books for children.

The Dinner Table

Dinnertime is an excellent opportunity to bring up ethical and moral issues. Sometimes an issue will appear in a family member's life or that of a friend or associate. Other times television or film will provide the topic. There also seem to be many opportunities in simply discussing current events. Bad examples oftentimes lead to the most interesting, revealing and helpful conversations.

I am more and more convinced that many of our problems could be solved if we would all just spend at least five dinners a week with our children—I mean quiet, civilized, unhurried dinners at a table. Whatever it is you have to give up to do this will most likely not be as important. In 1997, Bowden and Zeisz[29] reported that teens who ate dinner with their families an average of five days a week were more adjusted than teens who ate with their families only three times per week. Adjusted children were less likely to take drugs or be depressed, were more motivated at school, and had better relationships with their peers. The researchers noted that they did not know what aspect of the family mealtime, sharing, telling or hearing stories, was helpful in preventing adjustment problems. The researchers simply concluded that family mealtimes were strongly related to adjustment. When we sit daily (and when but at dinner time will this take place?) with our children and talk about things which are important to us and the decisions we have made and why, we teach and impart our values to our children. When we listen to their stories, we discover theirs. Whose opinions and values are more important to you? Our first job is to impart our values to our children over time in conversations that can take place anywhere. These tend to transpire at the table, on walks, at bedtime, or in any quiet, slow moment. Take time for your children and with your children. Be proactive not reactive.

Children are ours to win or lose. One of the most significant battlegrounds is the dinner table. Take the time. Win them here. As my friend Julie says—this may be asking for too much, but family breakfasts are great too. We do seem to have lost this fine art.

Countering Media Values

The downside to the media's involvement in our lives is that our children are bombarded by others' views and values in ways earlier generations were not. Countering this onslaught is an important part of our job. The media intrude into our lives through radio, television, film, video games, and the Internet. Programming and commercials send strong messages. The average child witnesses over 200,000 acts of violence on television by the time he is eighteen. He also spends 35 hours per week watching television and playing video games; this comprises almost a full-time job.[30]

Luckily, we can still control how much intrusion and what types of media are allowed in our homes, if we are willing and strong enough to do so. Television should never be on during family dinners or your children will take in the programs' values and perhaps miss the opportunities to learn yours. The vast majority of values on television clash loudly with traditional family values. On many television shows, dishonesty is rampant, respect nonexistent, self-restraint unheard of, and imprudent choices commonplace. Selfishness, immediate gratification, violence, and win-at-any cost are pervasive. Many of the children on television are not people I would want to live with nor have as neighbors. Life portrayed on much of television is frankly scary. Add to this the commercialism, materialism, and consumerism and you have a lot to contradict and invalidate.

David Walsh[31] asserts that children acquire values through observation, imitation, and trial and error interactions. Until 1950, this pattern of observation and imitation took place between significant and present adults and their children. Television has changed that and as a result has had an enormous impact on children's learning of values. Now, virtual adults and children, present only through media, are an integral part of the learning that takes place. Many children and teens spend far more time watching television people than real, live people, including family members. If we are not careful, if we fail to limit its influence, if we fail to take back our own influence, television will continue to be a prominent if not the sole teacher our children have.

Here are tips for reducing the harmful effects of TV:
1.   Limit television viewing. One hour per day is more than enough.

2.   Watch television together. Discuss what you see. Negative examples can be excellent teachable moments if you take the time to discuss why they are wrong.

3.   Establish clear rules and guidelines for what can be watched and when. Television programs now have ratings, as do movies. Use them and stick to them.

4.   Model good television viewing. Watch educational and informational programs. Limit channel surfing and pass-the-time watching. Choose another activity.

5.   Do not allow children under the age of 12 to watch the news live. It can be too intense, and you have no idea or control over what will be shown. It is one thing to hear about children shot at a school; it is another to watch bloody, wounded students carried out on gurneys.

6.   Keep television sets and computer screens out of children's rooms. This isolates children from the family. It also makes supervision of programming and viewing difficult.

7.   Preview or read a review of any movie or video before giving permission to your children to watch it.

8.   Provide and encourage other activities.

Television and other forms of media are not inherently bad. In fact, we now find ourselves able to find almost any necessary piece of information online from the comfort of our own homes. Education, both formal and informal, has received huge boosts from media. We can see actual footage of World War II, including some of the atrocities; seeing is believing and never forgetting. World news is available to us 24 hours a day if we like. We can review almost any book we want online, quickly and easily. Young people seem able to research anything online. We do not want the media to go away; they are far too valuable and useful to all of us. Nor can we expect the media to meet our needs; that is not their job. It is a business, they must be at least partially profit-driven. It is wonderful when they are family-values driven as well, but it is naive to expect this. Family values are our job. It is our responsibility as parents to use the control we have. And we have lots of power. First, we control what we tune into and purchase. If we stopped going to violent movies, they'd stop making them. It is that simple. Second, we control what our children witness and how much they partake. The control is in our hands. We just need to use it.

Consumerism

"What people call the spirit of the times is mostly their own spirit in which the times mirror themselves." —Johann Wolfgang von Goethe

Again in *Selling Out America's Children: How America Puts Profits Before Values and What Parents Can Do,* David Walsh notes that we must teach our children how advertising works and also how to counter its messages. Advertisers believe a child becomes a consumer by about age three. At three years, many children start making specific requests for brand-name products.[32] Marketers have aptly labeled children's influence and called it the nag factor.[33] Incidentally, many of the products targeted for the 4- to 12-year old age group have violence as a theme. All advertising is about buying and having. Advertisers are not evil people; they are simply doing the job of selling for their clients. We must nevertheless remember that if we allow them, they will shape our children's values, interests and behavior, and let's be honest, they do not have our children's best interests at heart. Their primary concern is selling, not our children's well-being. They are good at what they do. When you add up the financial resources, artistic talent, psychological and sociological knowledge, use of celebrity, technological advances and sheer number of advertising spots viewed, without our help, a child doesn't stand a chance.

How do our children get so caught up in consumerism and materialism? Brian Swimme in *The Hidden Heart of the Cosmos*,[34] states that before a child enters the 1st grade, he will have watched 30,000 advertisements. Jacobson and Mazur concur that children view somewhere between 20,000 to 40,000 television ads annually.[35] The time that teens spend absorbing ads is greater than their total stay in high school.[36] If we allow it, television and advertisers will have a tremendous influence on our children's values, desires, and thoughts. If we are not careful, our children will not even recognize the influence exerted upon them. Eventually we end up with a college student who has little idea how he has accrued the average $2250 in credit card debt.[37]

Walsh points out that long-lasting happiness cannot be found in material possessions; a consumerist culture promotes the notion that happiness can be found in material possessions. It is a strong message and needs countering. It is easy to become so preoccupied with material things that we tend to forget how to find our happiness in non-material ways.

Mary Pipher says that "this generation is the 'I want' generation. They have been educated to entitlement and programmed for discontent. Ads have encouraged this generation to have material expectations they can't fulfill."[38] As comedian George Carlin so humorously and wisely points out, we have too much "stuff." We spend the first part of our lives acquiring stuff, and the latter part of our lives trying to get rid of our stuff.

What can we do to counter consumerism?
1.   We must teach our children what advertising

is and what its purpose is: to make us want to buy something and to get us to run out and purchase it.

2. We must examine our own buying behavior and set limits on consumption. Do we have to have the very latest gadget, clothes, and automobile? Have we over-extended our credit? Do we save money regularly? Invest in our future? We must also model setting limits on consumption, ours and our children's.

3. Give your children an allowance. (Do not link it to chores; they do chores because they are part of the family, just as you do.) Let them learn how to waste or lose money and then how to spend, save, invest, and give wisely.

4. Spend twice as much *time* with your children and half as much *money* on them.[39] Trying to fulfill non-material needs with material things causes us to lose or miss contact with each other, with nature, and with our own playfulness.[40] It disrupts the connection between people.

5. Prioritize how you spend your time. Do you work all the time? Do you shop for fun and relaxation? Do you find free ways for your family to have fun?

6. Say no to unreasonable or constant requests or demands. In addition, teach and demonstrate the difference between need and want.

Please do not misunderstand. I am not suggesting that our children should not benefit from or enjoy the goods and services that our 21st century has to offer. Teaching our children the difference between "needs" and "wants" and how to create contentment in ways unrelated to consuming is a skill that will translate positively into many other areas of their lives. I might temporarily believe that I will feel so very much better if I am driving a brand new car: the truth is that I am the same person whether I am walking, riding, or driving. *I am responsible for the attitude I bring to each of my life experiences.*

Chapter Checkpoints

✔ Use stories to teach. Beware of and limit television and film; books frequently offer better alternatives.

✔ Have dinner with your children as often as you can. Make time to do this. Guard this time as valuable to their moral growth and your family time. Talk with them about their decisions and other bigger world decisions.

✔ Choose what type of influence all media have over your children. Limit the quantity. Have rules about television, video, and movie watching.

✔ Teach and enforce safe and appropriate Internet use.

✔ Watch, control and limit your own consumerism and materialism.

✔ Actively teach your children about advertising's power.

✔ Teach and practice delayed gratification.

Chapter Seven:
Children of Character

"Children have never been good at listening to their elders, but they have never failed to imitate them." —James Baldwin[41]

"[V]erbal lessons are important only to the degree that they are consistent with the ways your children see you behave."[42] —Steven C. Reuben

Rob had never been certain how he should act when he was in Michael's home: it was a place where people behaved so differently than in his own. Although the two houses were immediately next door to one another, and Rob could look directly into the bathroom and kitchen windows of Michael's home from his bedroom window, no two places could feel so different. Secretly, Rob was terrified of darkness and spent painfully long minutes during the night tossing and turning, imagining all manner of despicable and gruesome tortures which were sure to be visited upon him at any moment. If things were *that* bad at his house, how must they be at Michael's?

Michael's mother, you see, was a shrieker: nothing you did or said was responded to quietly. Mrs. Kablonski was downright scary. If they played in the backyard, they were "tearing up the grass," or making too much noise and she couldn't "hear her programs." If they played inside, they were also in the way: toy cars messed up the living room and forts in the basement hid all sorts of dangerous dust and dirt. If they talked to the dog, they were making the dog unhappy. If they were thirsty or hungry, they were interrupting her. Rob was often afraid of saying "good morning" just in case he had the facts wrong.

Michael's father, by contrast, seemed to be a gentle-spirited and kind man. When he was home on Saturday mornings, Rob and Michael watched cartoons with him and ate hot buttered toast with thick layers of jam; they washed these down with mugs of steamy hot chocolate with marshmallows melting on the top. Mr. Kablonski enjoyed hearing about their rambles in the woods, their imaginary enemies and games, and about their school yard frustrations. A dry-cleaner by profession, running a small town business, he knew many people in town and chatted amiably with most everybody they met when they were out for ice cream. But, as Rob grew older, he learned that there was a much darker side to Ed Kablonski.

In the evenings, after the boys were in bed, each in their own beds in their adjacent subdivision houses, Ed drank. Not just a beer over the evening hockey or football game on TV, but several glasses of straight whiskey one after another. And alcohol did not improve upon Ed's day. He was a nasty drunk: he hit Michael's mother and occasionally hauled Michael or one of his small brothers from their beds to berate them for their shortcomings. Michael's bleary-eyed mornings and bruised arms began to declare themselves more assertively as the boys grew older.

One particularly cold March day when they were twelve, Michael could barely stay awake at school; the day's arithmetic was beyond him, and he had been too tired to care much about the morning spelling test. Rob was worried and didn't know how to help. Walking home from school that afternoon, he thought he could convince Michael to do his work if he helped him with it. The thought that Michael might fail the year and they would find themselves separated in Sixth Grade was pricking him with a fretful worry. Inviting Michael into the house, Rob poured them each a glass of milk and raided the cookie stash his mother thought she had hidden on an upper shelf. Rob's mother, a school receptionist, wouldn't be home for another hour or so, and they were free to make themselves at home.

First up, Rob thought, they would get Michael's arithmetic homework done. Michael dozed on the sofa; Rob did the work and copied out a second sheet for Michael. It was while he was doing this that his mother walked through the door. Stopping to straighten his tousled hair and sigh at the sight of the entire bag of cookies gone, she puzzled over his homework activities. "Robbie," she said, picking up the second copies, "whose homework is this?" Michael continued to slumber peacefully; Rob looked up into his mother's face with gravity and reluctance.

"Mom, I have to do this for Michael, or he won't pass—trust me."

"Oh now, sweetheart, Michael's a bright boy," she said with confidence. "He's in no danger of failing." Glancing over at the sofa, she added with a frown, "He does, however, need to go to bed at a decent hour."

"But Mom. He does. He does, just like I do. But his...oh forget it. You wouldn't understand." Rob was annoyed, frustrated that his efforts to help were now, he was certain, foiled. Michael would fail and they would never be together again. He leapt to unreasonably grim and rapid conclusions, as twelve-year-olds will.

Sitting beside him at the table his mother tried to talk to him, her voice soothing and earnest. "Now, now, now...what exactly has you worried that Michael isn't going to make it? He's never seemed to have trouble at school before. Why would you be so worried?"

"Because he is too tired to get his work done...and sometimes I think that he doesn't care about school anymore. He doesn't talk to me as much as he used to, and he's too tired to even be any fun when he does." Worry and frustration spilled out in a torrent.

"Well now I'm starting to wonder what exactly is going on Robbie, what are you not telling me about? Why doesn't Michael sleep at night?" When her questions yielded no immediate answers, she spoke again, gently, "Robbie, you and I have a responsibility to think about what is best for Michael. As his friend you need to do what is right for him: that means not doing his homework for him because that is dishonest. But also, Rob, if you do the work, then Michael can't learn for himself how to answer the questions for when he is tested on it. Then he really will fail. Now, that doesn't mean that you can't help him to understand *how* to do the questions, it just means you can't encourage him to hand in work that is not his. That is wrong." She looked at Rob; Rob looked down, understanding how difficult this situation was becoming.

"Robbie, I think that there is something else worrying you. Let's talk about it so that we can help Michael together," she said.

Silence.

Rob's mother waited.

"Mom, it's not that easy," he whispered, his gaze sweeping over Michael's sleeping form.

"Mom, sometimes things aren't so nice at Michael's house. Sometimes his dad...oh, you know Michael's dad, he's great to us on Saturdays. But he's not always nice," he said, his voice falling even lower. "Mom, sometimes he drinks too much I think. He gets Michael and Ben and Larry up in the night. He shouts and...he hurts them. When I go to bed at night I worry about scary things happening, but I think that at Michael's house they really do happen."

Rob's Mom looked over at Michael sadly. The child slept blissfully on, cuddled up against the quilted cushions, deaf to his secrets now revealed.

"Rob, I am so glad that you told me about this. Michael needs you to tell the truth. Rob, this is a problem that children can't solve by themselves: adults have to help. No matter how unhappy or angry or drunk he is, Mr. Kablonski does not have the right to hurt anybody." Leaning his chest and head against his mother's shoulder, Rob felt a wave of relief wash over him, years of worry and anxiety dripping from his arms and chest.

"I won't lie to you, Rob," she said, holding him firmly in her arms, "it won't be pleasant. But we will get Michael and his brothers some help. You have done the right thing."

What questions do we need to ask ourselves if we are to help children of character to develop? Steven Carr Reuben in *Children of Character: A Parent's Guide*[43] suggests the following questions: What kind of person do you want your child to grow up to be? What kind of human being will he or she become? What qualities do you most want to nurture in them? What must you do to create this? Developing character takes planning. It should not be left up to chance.

Clear Values and Standards

Perhaps the first thing we parents need to do is to make a list of our core values. What characteristics or virtues do we most want to see in ourselves and our children? This is called planning. Too often it appears that parents spend more time planning their grocery lists or vacations than they do planning their children's upbringing. If we are not certain about where we are heading and take direct, concrete steps to get there, life will most certainly take us wherever it chooses. We very much need to be the masters of our destiny with regard to parenting and character development. What characteristics or abilities would give you the most satisfaction to see in your children years from now, as adults, as spouses, as parents?

Norman Vincent Peale named seven traits: honesty, courage, enthusiasm, service, faith, hope and love. William Bennett in his *Book of Virtues*[44] and *The Moral Compass*[45] suggested ten: self-discipline, compassion, responsibility, friendship, work, courage, perseverance, honesty, loyalty, and faith. Make a list of your own "hoped-fors," and then pare it down to something manageable, ten or twelve, to get to your core values. In families where there are two parents, you will need to compare and pool your lists and eventually come up with a combined list. Finding ways to agree can be difficult; however, if you send conflicting messages to your child (one parent believes and acts upon religion being an important, daily part of life and the other parent gives religion no part of his), you will confuse the child. Finding ways to respect and honor each other's core values provides excellent modeling for problem solving, team playing, and the give and take of conflict resolution.

Your children need you to have clear values and clear standards. Clear communication with matching action will be required as well. I cannot stress this enough. Being a role model for your children is neither optional nor arbitrary. Being a character model and a model of integrity (matching your beliefs and words to your actions) is not easy. It is not comfortable either. Children notice everything, especially those things we wish they did not. There is no tricking children; don't even try if your child is over two years of age. They catch it all and record it for later use. Ask any parent of teens. What is it we can do to model character effectively for our children?

Do the Right Thing

"Don't worry that children never listen to you. Worry that they are always watching you." —Robert Fulghum

It sounds so incredibly simple, and conceptually it is clear. All we need to do is choose to do the right things. Hopefully, we all know right from wrong. Actually doing it, acting right, consistently and continuously, is dismayingly difficult. It requires constant vigilance, and the willingness and ability to hold ourselves and our emotions in check.

We will have to learn to:
1. Act as though someone is always watching, like your mother, a rabbi, minister or priest.
2. Make acting right an ordinary part of everyday life. It is found in small gestures and respectful remarks: allowing the car who has been waiting for the parking spot but is blocked by the car leaving to have the spot that was fairly theirs, or speaking kindly and respectfully to all persons, regardless of their station or ability to do something for you.
3. Choose to do right over the long term. One cannot simply make right choices on weekends or for a few months. "Character, after all, is a long-term project."[46]

4.   Choose friends who act right. Remember that every adult who you bring into your child's life will project, consciously or unconsciously, why your child should be like him. Our children seem to be such quick studies on this subject. Many parents find it amazing that behavior in friends that did not bother them prior to having children suddenly seems very distressing and disturbing after. The quick haphazard racial slur once ignored now seems offensive and too glaring to overlook. Friendships sometimes fade or shift after the birth of a child. No child has small ears or small eyes.

5.   Be the kind of friend you would want your child to be. Do you belittle a friend who is not present? Do you take from the friendship but never give? What is the purpose of your friendship? Thirty-three percent of teens have not done a favor for free for anyone in the previous month.[47]

The following is a quick review of this section.

1.   Make a list of your core values.

2.   The struggle to build and maintain character is lifelong. As difficult as determining and listing our core values is, practicing them is even more challenging.

3.   When deciding what to model, ask yourself one of four questions:

1)   What is the right thing to do?

2)   What would I wish that my child would do in this situation?

3)   What would I wish that my child's spouse would do in this situation? If the first two don't get you, this will.

4)   "When this moment is over and I'm looking back on it in the future, will I be proud of the person I was and what I did?"[48]

Virtues

Recently, a good deal has been written about virtues and values. For the purposes of this book, we are going to define these two terms. Values are opinions, generally opinions regarding controversial issues such as: abortion, capital punishment, what form God takes, how the world came to be, or as mundane as the consumption of alcohol or whether it is better to live in the city or the country. As a society, we vary widely on these. Some people prefer to think of them as issues. Virtues, on the other hand, are life skills which enhance any life. These include prudence, fortitude, temperance, perseverance, etc. No one disagrees about these. Some people prefer to call these values. The difficulty with this is that they can then be confused with the issues, or what many people call values as listed above.

This differing use of the word values has caused confusion, especially with regard to the role of teachers. Public school teachers are not allowed to teach values or, in other words, opinions on issues. This is correct. It is unfair for me, your child's teacher, to use my position and status as his teacher to promote my viewpoint or value on abortion. This should make any parent edgy. You don't know what my value or opinion is, and it could quite easily differ from yours. It is a parent's job, and a parent's job only, to teach values. I will teach my children my viewpoint, my values, regarding abortion, God, capital punishment, etc. No teacher has that right. These are called *family values* for a reason. When we realized that we had become a heterogeneous nation rather than a homogeneous one, we realized that an individual family's values took precedence.

Our error was to throw the baby out with the bath water; in other words, we also stopped teaching virtues. We did not need to do that, nor was this helpful to the development of good character in our children. No one has a concern about me, or any of your child's teachers, teaching any child fortitude or perseverence, the ability to hang in when the going gets tough. This can only help a child. There is no controversy or disagreement about teaching a child prudence, the ability to make wise and kind choices, based on positive outcomes. This, too, can only make the child's life and the world better. Values we have discussed; the dinner table was a primary tool in teaching values. It is now time to discuss virtues; dinner table conversations remain a wonderful technique for teaching these as well. There are also a host of other tools available.

How do we teach virtues? First, we must be aware of them. When I ask groups of parents or teachers to name virtues, there is sometimes real difficulty in naming them. If we want to teach our children to be virtuous, perhaps we should first start with knowing virtues and their opposites, vices. There are many resources and curriculum-type guides already available; seek out the ones you find agreeable. One of my favorite resources is Margaret Anderson who discusses four cardinal virtues: prudence, fortitude, justice and temperance, and some tips for teaching them to children.[49] These are a wonderful starting point for the development of good character. The starred tips are Mrs. Anderson's.

PRUDENCE is the ability to govern and discipline oneself by the use of reason. It may be taught by parents or other adults in a child's life, and it requires maturity. Generally, it comes with age and practice, and allows us to choose actions which lead to real happiness.

1.   Use discipline to teach children to choose correct/moral principles and actions. Do not

shy away from the lessons.

2. Teach children to think through to outcomes when making decisions about how they will behave. Help them to see that the outcome is far longer lasting than the behavior.

3. Work repeatedly with the child who makes impulsive decisions; continue to show her how heedless, undirected behavior frequently ends up being a poor decision.*

4. Teach clear thinking. Explain the reasoning behind some of your own decisions and actions. Ask children why they made certain decisions. Model stop and think.

5. I confess I am biased, but television tends to offer opportunities for discussion of imprudent decisions. Books generally portray wiser decisions.

FORTITUDE is courage and staying power. It is the strength of mind that enables one to bear adversity.

1. Practice patience during delays and grace during disappointments.* I witness grownups who have neither of these virtues; just ask any gate agent at the airport. I am also seeing more and more children who are given their own way and have not learned that life will not always go their way nor how to handle these times with maturity and grace.

2. Avoid overindulgence like the plague. Do not give in to a child's every whim and desire.*

3. Help children learn to persevere.* Chosen activities such as baseball, piano lessons, and dance are excellent vehicles. Persist, unless you chose the activity for them. Finishing tasks and chores also contributes to the development of fortitude or persistence.

4. Look for the good in others and in situations; even the worst situations and problems tend to teach very important lessons.
5. Guide children toward self-reliance. It is our job to help them grow away from us, physically, socially, and emotionally. Give them the skills to do so expertly. We must remember to balance this lesson with the equally important lesson of interdependence and connection.

JUSTICE is the ability to treat others fairly, and to look after the rights of others, even those absent. It means giving each his due.

1. Teach children to stand up against injustice to themselves and others.* When a child feels a teacher has treated her unfairly, help her write a respectfully descriptive note to help the teacher understand her perspective. Role play the discussion and then let your child handle the discussion with the teacher. Teach children to address injustice to others, especially those weaker.
2. Show respect to all, even during times of anger. Remember, use respectful language.
3. Teach and expect honesty. Be honest; never ask a child to lie for you. ("Tell him I'm not here." Ring a bell for you?)
4. Make and keep promises.*
5. Deal with stealing, cheating, lying, and manipulation as they occur. Name them.
6. Teach impartiality. Handle your children impartially—no favoritism. Deal with others impartially without regard to race, religion, social status, or gender.*
7. Teach them to judge themselves, not others.

8. Teach generosity, but intelligent generosity.*
   Overindulgence is not intelligent generosity.
   Give others their due and then some.*

9. Teach "please" and "thank you" and other
   courtesies not so common these days.
   Demonstrate, practice, and then expect
   friendliness and kindness; everyone deserves
   these.

10. Practice problem solving, negotiation skills
    and conflict resolution—over and over and
    over again.

TEMPERANCE is moderation or self-control, the ability
to limit or check oneself.

1. Help children learn to handle their emotions.
   Time-out is most helpful. Also, never allow
   tears, outbursts, or tantrums to get a child what
   he wants. Replace these uncivilized
   behaviors with more civilized actions, such as
   removing oneself to a quiet place, counting to
   ten, taking a deep breath, and learning
   respectful language, especially descriptive
   language.

2. Know and enforce true limits. Drinking may
   be alright, as is driving, but both are age-
   dependent. Drinking and driving together are
   never alright. Hurting others with words or
   fists is not alright.

3. Build self-esteem, but also teach humility,
   "the virtue that makes it possible for a man to
   know the truth about himself."[50]

4. Making things *right* is fine; getting even is
   not.

5. Learn to recognize your own warning bells.
   Listen to them and act on them.

6. Seek balance in life. Limit television. A

television, video game or computer with or without Internet capability does not belong in a child's bedroom. Put these in a general, supervised area of the house so you know what they are seeing and doing. Otherwise, children can isolate themselves. Limit outside activities to ensure family time.

7.   Teach that more is not necessarily better.

One of the most important parts of teaching virtues is making clear that when we make decisions about our behavior, we must look at the outcomes of the behavior, not simply the behavior or temptation. Choosing between outcomes rather than behaviors leads to responsible, prudent, virtuous, in other words, right choices. Putting long-term goals over short-term needs can be difficult, but generally leads to a far better life, in every sense of the word. These virtues so tough to come by are also so beneficial—and beautiful to witness.

We were off to lunch—one of those rare days when both my college-age sons were available while I was in their college town. The day boded bright, and fun was on the horizon. We came to a stoplight. As we waited, a car came around the adjacent corner and as the driver turned, his car door suddenly flew open. The driver grabbed his door of course, but in the process, veered right and sideswiped a parked car. To our amazement, he righted the door to his car and sped off.

"Did you see that?" Chris asked.

Mike responded, "Yeah, he rammed right into that car. Go after him: we need his license plate number." The light turned green and we followed. As we caught up to the car, Mike and I got his number.

"Mom, where's your cell phone? We need to call the cops."

"Never mind, there's one right there." To my amazement, a police car loomed just ahead of us. How many times have I asked myself, where are they when you need them? And here was one when I needed one.

Mike, who was on the side next to the police car, rolled down his window and explained quickly what we had just witnessed. The officer asked if we had gotten the license plate number. Mike gave it to him, described the car, and told him what street the culprit had just turned down. The officer nodded, "I'll go find him."

Chris turned the car around at the next corner announcing, "I need to go back and leave a note on that car. Whoever owns it may need a witness." Back we went. Finishing our final deed, we belatedly but happily headed for the restaurant.

How amazing, not only had these guys thought very quickly (they could describe both cars and knew which street the miscreant had gone down), they had also known what to do. They had known the right things to do and had done them without hesitation. Good kids. The world is a better place because of what had just taken place. The Law of the Harvest came briefly to mind. Sometimes what we see in our children pains us or scares us; sometimes it reaffirms and contents us.

Helpful Questions

✔ Ask yourself:
1. What kind of person do I want my child to grow up to be?

2. What qualities do I most want to develop or nurture?

✔ Teach them to ask themselves:
1. Would I be comfortable telling my mother or father what I did?

2. Would I rather that other people did not know what I had done?

3. Will I be proud of the person I was and what I did?

4. What would the world be like if everyone acted the way I do?

5. What would I want done if I were the other person, if the situation were reversed?

Chapter Checkpoints

✔ Know your core values, and actively teach and live them. Plan what character traits you wish to give your children.

✔ Do right, and choose friends who do so as well.

✔ Teach and practice virtues.

✔ Teach your children to make behavioral decisions based on outcomes: "What could possibly happen if I do this?"

✔ Our children are ours to win or lose. We must sometimes fight ourselves to win, but they are worth the struggle. It is time for us to get it right.

Chapter Eight:
Discipline & Character Development

Exhausted, Mary Anne climbed wearily up the outside apartment stairs. Bits of grit, dust and leaf scraped beneath her shoes, reminding her that there was sweeping to be done. With a sigh she rummaged through her bag for her keys, shifting the briefcase awkwardly to her other arm. The keys somehow could never be found, even five minutes after being deposited. The lines on her face deepened; she closed her eyes prayer-like, her newly graying hair blowing in the evening breeze. Opening her eyes she caught sight of a small chickadee flitting on the deck railing. Turning her gaze back to the bag, she dug into it. The key emerged seconds later and she opened the apartment door.

Walking directly into the kitchen she discovered that the children had been there before her. The counter was littered with a variety of sizes of sticky knives and bread crumbs. The bag of bagels lay open beside this and an empty carton of orange juice tipped on its side beside that. The morning breakfast dishes were still stacked higgledy piggledy beside the sink. In the gloomy light she could hear the television sounds of canned laughter. This was all to be expected, she supposed. She had always known that being on her own with the kids would add to her already weighty responsibilities, but there were days when she just could not face another task, no matter how insignificant. When her survey revealed a carton of milk sitting on top of the fridge, she closed her eyes again.

How many times had she told them that the milk needed refrigeration? Now an extra trip out to get fresh would be required. And what about the waste of her already meager resources? She pinched her eyes tighter and raised her hands to her face, dropping her bags with a clatter to the floor. A tightness spread across her chest and around to the muscles in her upper back and neck. She raked her hands above her eyes and up into her ragged hairline.

A small and gentle gesture at her feet broke through the spring-tight silence. The dog, a small, rather unattractive creature of indeterminate breed, sat quietly at her feet with tail wagging, waiting patiently for an opportunity to greet her.

How we discipline our children is inextricably linked to their developing character. There seems to be so much confusion regarding what is and is not discipline. Although this author has thoroughly discussed discipline in *Discipline for Life: Getting it Right with Children*, a short discussion of discipline is called for in this chapter.

The word discipline means to teach. It does not mean to take away or hurt (punishment), to bribe and buy off our children (rewards), nor to control their behavior (power). The word itself suggests that when children misbehave, and they will, that a parent's job is to teach them what they need to learn. Interestingly, it is a child's misbehavior which guides us to the needed lesson. We grownups need children to misbehave in order to give us clues as to what we need to teach them. For example, when a sister shoves her brother because he colored on her paper, she needs to be taught effective words to use that prevent or stop his drawing on her paper. Try, "If you're going to color on my paper, you'll have to sit somewhere else." She has the right to protect her paper, a lesson she has already learned or known from birth; she does not have the right to use aggression to solve this problem. On the other hand, her brother's misbehavior, drawing on someone else's paper without permission, suggests that he needs to learn that he needs permission to do this and that he is going to have to learn how to keep his crayon to his own drawing when he does not receive permission. He may have been trying to make friends with his sister and need better friendship building skills like offering her a crayon, smiling and saying hi, or he may need to learn some impulse control—one simply does not get to do whatever one wants. It is their misbehavior which tells us that each needs lessons and directs us to those lessons.

Where we have made our largest mistake with regard to discipline is that we have failed for several generations to hold in mind that every time we discipline a child we are not only teaching life skills and appropriate lessons, we are also teaching guiding life principles. Integrity is required.

Guiding Life Principles
Guiding life principles are the means or methods by which a child will make decisions about her behavior for the rest of her life. If teaching these sounds like a huge responsibility, it is. It frightens me. If this sounds new, it is not. In fact, you already know this. Each of us has witnessed and recognized that what we do with children when they are young, returns—to help us or haunt us—as they age into adolescence and adulthood. This is called the Law of the Harvest: it states that we reap what we sow. Let's begin with the sowing aspect.

It is quite clear that we want our children to choose to do the right thing; however, what motivates a child to do the right thing is as important as that he chooses to do it. In fact, in terms of character development and integrity, why a child makes his behavioral choice determines good and bad, weak or strong character. The "why" of his choice, the reasoning behind it, is the guiding life principle. Let us look at a few illustrative examples.

One mother told me about how she'd had it with her children being ugly to each other. Although she really wasn't too keen, she decided to set up a reward system where they got points (toward buying a desired toy) each time they were nice or kind to each other or looked after each other. Immediately kind acts began to happen. She was so pleased. This is the choosing to do the right thing part. Don't we all want our children to be kind to others? However, before the end of the day, she noticed a new pattern of behavior. Prior to any child doing anything for a sibling, he would run to her and ask if this particular act qualified for the points. Needless to say, if the act did not qualify, the child chose not to be nice in this way. There were no good Samaritans being developed here. There were only paid acts of kindness. No warmth of spirit or solidifying of connections was taking place. These children had quite quickly learned that one should be paid for kindness. As with all reward systems, these children learned and practiced the guiding life principle, "What will I get if I choose to do this?" or in other words, "What's in it for me?" The question a parent must ask herself is do I want my child to guide her behavior by what others will "pay" (with token, sticker, money, privilege, affection) her to do. The answer to that is a resounding no. What is the difference between rewarding and bribing? Conceptually, what is the difference between my giving a young child a sticker or a star or a privilege to put her shoes on quickly so we can leave and get to the doctor's office on time, and my paying $25,000 to an employee in another company to bring me a computer disk with all of the client files, complete with phone numbers and addresses? There is no difference.

Why do we want a child to choose to do the right thing? More precisely, what do we want to be the child's *reason* for making his behavioral choice? Let me be very clear. We want children to choose to do the right thing not because they will get something, not because there is something in it for them. We want children, as well as adults, to choose to do the right thing *simply and only because it is the right thing.* That means we must discipline them in ways which teach them to ask the questions, "Is this a right or wrong thing to do?" and "What could possibly happen to me if I choose to do this?" We cannot buy good behavior and expect good character to develop. We must indeed put our children first; we will have to let rewards go as a means of dealing with and disciplining our children.

Punishment, as opposed to discipline, is another method we will have to abandon. Briefly, punishment includes all of the ugly words we use with our children (belittling, putting-down), any hitting, striking or spanking, and the taking away of unrelated privileges. Punishment is based on a principle that says that I have the right to hurt you (emotionally, socially, physically or financially) if I do not like or approve of your behavior. First, this is a principle that will return to haunt us; as they grow older, our children most likely will not approve of our behavior. Do they then have the right to harm us? Secondly, it is a faulty principle; we do not have the right to hurt one another because we disagree—even with behavior. When children are punished rather than disciplined, they learn to determine if they are willing to pay the price for a misbehavior. If they are, they can go ahead and digress and pay and then be even again. It is a transaction. Thus, one may choose to do the wrong thing, as long as one pays for the digression. It is not alright to do wrong things—ever. And better still for the digressor under punishment, if one does not get caught, one does not even have to pay; one simply gets away with doing wrong.

For example, if a five-year-old hits her younger brother for taking some of her play dough, and her father takes her *unrelated* television privileges away, he teaches her that he will hurt her in some way when she does wrong. He will make her pay for her misbehavior; she loses television viewing for a night, an unrelated privilege. Instead, he could sit and teach her problem-solving skills (how to keep her brother out of her play dough by having some ready to give to him when he arrives at her play table) so that she can solve this type of problem with her brother civilly, or he can remove her from her brother. There she loses the *related* privilege of playing with him and staying in the same room with him. Father may also choose to work with his younger son (depending on his age) and teach him how to ask for play dough and how to wait patiently for a little while as his sister finds some for him. Both children will need to be taught one of their job descriptions as siblings: you need to get along. You may disagree, but do so agreeably.[51] I am not suggesting that children are always happy when we discipline them rather than punish them. What I am suggesting is that punishment's goal is simply to cause pain; discipline's goal is to teach. It is a subtle difference, but an important one. In the next chapter we will examine how evil carries within its definition the deliberate causing of harm and injury.

And lastly, if we choose to get our children to behave by force, either brute physical force or verbal wrangling, we teach them to behave only when others can make them. Thus, when there is no one around to make you do right, you may do whatever you wish, like when there are no police around, and you want to speed; or when you are at college, and no one makes you go to class or do homework; or when your mom is upstairs and you and your brother are downstairs and you want his cookie. No one is there to make you do right, and no one will ever know the truth. Controlling our children leads them as far away from the goal of all discipline—self-discipline—as any system. Character is determined by one's ability to choose to do right on one's own, when no one is looking and no one will make you. Clearly, many lessons will be required. It is our job to ensure that these take place.

It is important then for us to determine what is discipline and what is not, what leads our kids to solid character and what leads them astray. We are responsible for finding out and knowing, and we are not allowed to blame the experts for telling us otherwise. *You* determine how you handle your children's misbehavior and you and no one else owns this. If we are going to hold the children accountable for their behavior, we must start by holding ourselves accountable for ours. We must first get it right with our children before they can get it right with themselves. For additional insight into discipline and for discipline strategies, please see *Discipline for Life: Getting it Right with Children.*

We need to get our principles correct when we discipline and only teach and model the principles we believe. This, of course, is integrity again, practicing only what we believe. Sometimes we fail at an even more basic level—we fail to address misbehavior, rudeness, insensitivity, and indifference. These missteps, too, develop a type of character, but sadly it is poor character.

Because I travel so much and visit so many different places, I often find myself with the opportunity to observe people in a variety of settings. I come away with stories which both validate the work of parents and educators, but also remind me of what still needs attention.

As I stood in a church lobby one evening waiting for my session on discipline to begin, I had the opportunity to relax and watch the comings and goings of a busy church congregation. It was more than twenty minutes before my program's start, and only a few parents had arrived. At the same time, young adults were arriving for their own evening programs. Abruptly, a sixteen or seventeen year old girl walked up to the glass double doors, a cell phone to her ear. She pulled on one door's handle and found the door locked. Annoyance and impatience immediately crossed her face. She looked in and seeing me standing there, pounded on the door and eyed me crossly. I got up and opened it, despite the fact that everyone else had, on their own, discovered that the adjacent second door was unlocked. Walking through while I held the door, she continued her phone conversation, never once making eye contact, smiling a thank you, nor verbally acknowledging my help. It was if I did not exist and perhaps I had ceased to exist the moment I had fulfilled her need. My first thought was that surely someone had missed teaching this girl manners, common courtesies, or that she had failed to learn them. She was quite rude. In truth, I know nothing about her character, but my brief experience of her gives me no reason at all to put faith in her character.

It is such a small thing, saying thank you, making eye contact, or waving appreciation. Yet, more and more frequently I meet "this girl" on the street. I allow her to cross in front of my car, she does not acknowledge my courtesy; I hold a door, she says nothing in response. How much does a smile cost? How much does eye contact and a nod cost? Is a thank you that much trouble? I am beginning to wonder. I do know this—as a nation, we are starting to look bad.

Chapter Checkpoints

✔ Discover what is discipline and what is not. Get it right in your head so you can get it right with your children.

✔ Teach only Guiding Life Principles that are correct.

✔ Children's misbehavior tells us what lessons to teach them.

✔ Teach children not just to do the right thing but to do the right thing simply and only because *it is the right thing.*

✔ Remember the Law of the Harvest.

✔ Manners and courtesies are so easy to perform, and they make life so much nicer. Where have they gone?

Chapter Nine:
Bad Character

When it Goes Wrong: Evil

It may seem strange, but it also seems necessary in a book about developing good character that we discuss what constitutes bad character. Indeed, it is helpful to know which traits we do not wish to encourage in our children, just as it is important to know what constitutes poor discipline. There are many unhelpful methods of child instruction and correction which we all wish to avoid.

Let us begin by examining the similarities between the meanings of wrong, bad and evil. The dictionary[52] defines wrong as *injurious, unfair, unjust and immoral conduct, and a willingness to cause harm without due provocation or just cause.* The definition of bad includes *below standard morally, evil, injurious, and harmful.* Evil has the most sinister connotation yet includes many of the same descriptors and overtones: *wicked, not good morally, arising from bad character and behavior, and causing harm.* The point here is that bad character, wrongdoing and evil are quite related and somewhat synonymous. When we talk about one, we are talking about them all. All involve causing harm, being unfair, doing injustice, or lacking morality. Yet it is really only evil that we shun and which frightens us. Perhaps we are a bit shortsighted about this.

The Continuum of Evil

None of us wants to consider ourselves evil. Although we may on occasion do wrong or bad things, we are not evil. Evil people are someone else—something other than us, separate from us, less than us. Evil, however, may be just at the far end of a continuum of wrong, injurious, and unjust acts. Yes, clearly there are different sizes of evil: nabbing someone's parking spot is nowhere near putting your two sons in your car and pushing it into a lake or blowing up a federal building in Oklahoma City. The question to ask ourselves is, "Where do I draw the line?" We all have a spot on the continuum; I know no one who always chooses to do what is right and moral. We all seem to have a point where minimally acceptable behavior moves into minimally unacceptable behavior. For example, we may accept disrespectful yelling at our children but not hitting them. We exceed the speed limit by 10 miles per hour, but not by 20. Some of us set that limit at 5 miles per hour, others at 30. Many of us would kill to protect ourselves or our children, but not for any other reason. At least that is what we believe. How does one know until tested? Farther out on the continuum, however, is what we consider to be true evil—behavior we hope we or our children never commit, the kind that only those whose world view is radically different from ours would ever consider doing, serial killing, pedophilia, for example.

Nurturing Evil

Newsweek[53] magazine reports that scholars from psychology, sociology, philosophy and theology have found that most of us do indeed have the capacity, not a proclivity, for doing horrific evil. This makes one wonder what goes into creating someone who is capable of committing huge evils? What as parents should we avoid like the plague? Psychiatrist Michael Wedner of the New York University School of Medicine reported to the American Psychiatric Association that evil generally includes an intent to cause emotional trauma, to terrorize and target the helpless, to prolong suffering and to derive satisfaction from all of this. Many evildoers lack the capacity for empathy; they do not understand in their hearts or heads the pain and terror felt by

another human being. The article, however, cautioned that
while a failure of empathy may be a
sufficient cause of evil, it is not a necessary
one: sociopaths often know full well what
their victims feel, and revel in it. To be truly
evil seems to require a void where compassion
should be: an evildoer like a serial sexual
killer knows full well, but does not care a
whit, what another feels.[54]
The ability to dehumanize others also appears to be an
important factor. Ted Bundy called his 24 female victims
"cargo" and "damaged goods." Timothy McVeigh called the
children he killed "collateral damage." There also appears to
be a component of narcissism or self-centeredness coupled
with grandiosity. It has been suggested that narcissism is the
trait that allows seemingly ordinary people to commit evil
acts. Feelings of grandiosity allow one to make decisions
about who lives and dies or who suffers.

Other experts argue that nurture or environment
contributes to bad character. Dr. Carl Goldberg, a
psychoanalyst at the Albert Einstein College of Medicine in
New York, who has long studied killers and sociopaths, notes
that if a child suffers extreme neglect or cruelty the result will
often be shame and humiliation. It is worse when the
suffering occurs at the hands of trusted relatives or friends.
These feelings of unworthiness, if not countered by
compassion from others in the child's life, can grow into a
profound self-contempt. This self-contempt must, for
survival, be turned into an indifference towards others and
their feelings. This indifference becomes, says Goldberg, "I
may not be worthy, but neither is anyone else."[55]

In addition, abuse appears to leave a physical trace on
the child's brain. The brain is assaulted with stress hormones
which cause the child to become inured to stress and to

feeling. He has no emotions and this is translated to others not having any either. Not only does this child not feel his own feelings, he cannot perceive or feel anyone else's either. "One of the most consistent findings about the biology of violence is that sadists and cold-blooded killers show virtually no response to stress—no racing heart, no sweating, no adrenaline rush." Children cannot handle a constant barrage of stress; we are obliged to try to reduce and minimize their stressors, not augment and cause them.

It must be noted here that abuse and neglect may be emotional with no physical component. A child who is never struck but frequently told she is worthless, bad and irritating is abused. Parents can be physically present with a child and emotionally distant or absent; this is neglect. A child need not *be* alone to *feel* alone. In this world of busy-ness, running around and parental self-interest, increasing numbers of children who have parents do not have adequate parenting.

In addition, evil can spring from ideas rather than feelings. " 'You can have people who have a well-developed capacity for empathy, relating, who are very close to their friends, but who have been raised in an ideology that teaches them that people of another religion, color or ethnic group are bad,' says psychologist Bruce Perry of the Child Trauma Academy in Houston. 'They will act in a way that is essentially evil based upon cognition rather than emotion.' "[56] Of course, the heart and head do interact and thus those brought up with neglect and abuse are more susceptible to ideologies which dehumanize or demonize others.

Another disturbing component of evil was well illustrated in 1974 by researcher Stanley Milgram.[57] His studies proved that the desire to conform was a powerful component in the descent towards harmful conduct. Dr. Milgram placed volunteers in front of a panel of (fake) electrical switches believed to be connected to other volunteers, the "learners." The first volunteers, with the switches, were told that the effect of electric shock on learning was being tested. When the learner got an answer wrong, he was to be shocked by the volunteer. Each time a wrong answer occurred, the volunteer was to throw a more powerful switch. When alone, more than 50% administered the maximum and potentially fatal 450-volt shock even as they heard victims scream in (mock) agony. When the volunteers were seated between two others (associates of Milgram) who showed no qualms about torturing the learners, 92% administered the potentially lethal shocks. They simply complied with directions, they followed orders. These results are horrifying but also enlightening.

Even while understanding and noting all of these factors, we still fail fully to explain evil. There are thousands upon thousands of people with these traits or family configurations who do not commit atrocities, who like all of us, commit "trivial evils" (cutting someone off in traffic) but go no further. Clearly, generalities help us understand what to avoid in our upbringing of children but do not fully explain evildoing. For now, we are just not smart enough to know or to predict which child will be the one. We can only consider and learn in hindsight and perhaps avoid any of the potential contributing factors.

We must also remember that children's brains are not fully developed; even at the onset of puberty, major brain construction and configuring are taking place. Moral judgment, the ability to determine right from wrong, and moral motivation, the desire to put the rights and needs of others above our own, often elude children. However, the moral stage of development of Eric Harris of Columbine High School need not have been permanent. The tragedy is that he acted brutally before this stage was outgrown or detected. Let this be a lesson to us all: children require guidance, modeling, teaching and supervision. This is a gravely important part of our job as parents. None of us can afford to overlook it, to be too busy or too self-involved to notice it. My question is this: how did Susan Smith arrive at adulthood, give birth to two children, and be able to dispatch them with the justification that, "I love my children with all my heart. My children deserve to have the best, and now they will."[58] She failed to mention that she had a boyfriend who, she thought, would marry her if she did not have the encumbrance of children.

The danger in trying to explain evil is that we move towards accepting the concept of predestination. Are there just certain personality types and certain life experiences which cause evildoing? Just because we can explain and understand what went wrong with someone does not mean we can rationalize or excuse what they have done. They had a choice and they made one. The purpose of looking at the origins of evil is to avoid any potential pitfalls. We do not want to contribute to our children embracing attitudes and behaviors which they cannot control.

Chapter Checkpoints

✔ Wrong, bad and evil are each positions on the same continuum. Each includes causing harm and doing wrong.

✔ A lack of empathy, the absence of compassion, a sense of grandiosity and the ability to dehumanize others may contribute to the ability to do evil to others.

✔ Abuse or neglect can produce profound self-loathing and indifference to others.

✔ A fairly constant stream of stress, as produced by abuse or neglect, may lead to the numbing of feelings and the inability to read one's own emotions or those of others. These people exhibit a lack of empathy.

✔ Ideologies which assert that select groups of people are subhuman or somehow wrong allow for and encourage the growth of the dehumanization component.

✔ Condoning by others seems to make evil easier to commit.

✔ The ability to determine right from wrong and the desire to do right develop throughout childhood and adolescence. These must be taught and nurtured into fruition.

✔ Doing right or doing wrong is always a choice.

Chapter Ten:
Running Against the Grain

After a long day of classes and waiting on tables, Laura was exhausted. Her lower back ached and her ankles and feet felt swollen with overuse. The restaurant had too many stairs; admittedly each shift offered a free workout without the nagging trainer, but after an already full day it felt more like a feat of endurance. Walking in the November chill down the block to the corner grocery store, Laura mentally wrote out her list and compared it with the cash she carried; hopefully, she had enough.

The grocery store's staff seemed to turn over regularly, and as Laura searched the aisles for the spice she needed and collected her bread, milk and laundry soap, she overheard the store's night manager gruffly training a new recruit. The new clerk, clearly a recent immigrant to the country, looked ashen. The challenge of unfamiliar money, new language and weighty responsibility was taking its toll.

Laura carried her items up to the counter and smiled. "Hi," she said, and added: "Gray day, isn't it?"

"Yes, yes," the clerk replied, turning the items over and over, attempting to find the prices. His hands shook and, clumsily, he moved from one item to the next. Laura's face reflected a conflicting mixture of emotion: amusement, caution, concern and indifference. When he had calculated her total she realized in an instant that he had miscalculated $10 in her favor, a $10 bonus that her budget could certainly use. Sighing softly with wistful regret she turned to him.

"There's been a mistake. I owe you $10 more than you asked me for. It's easy to goof these things up when you are new to them. Let me help you with the prices."

Later, as she walked home along the damp and gritty pavement, she thought of his anxious and overly effusive thanks for her honesty. It had been a long day, but she walked face forward, heart full and head wise.

Moral Authority

"I simply did the right thing as much as I could."[59] —Ken Barun

"Moral authority belongs to those who are willing to write their signature on their lives."[60] —Eugene Kennedy and Sara Charles

"We are what we seem." —William Galin, 20th Century American psychiatrist

Authority or authorship is a critical concept to rearing our children. We sometimes misunderstand it and oftentimes confuse it with authoritarianism. Authority is a *positive, dynamic force ordered to growth.*[61] "Authority's essentially dynamic character is obvious from its root, shared with 'author' and 'augment,' in the Latin *augere*: 'to create, to enlarge, to make able to grow.' Authority generates life."[62] In *Authority: The Most Misunderstood Idea in America,* Kennedy and Charles suggest that

> morality cannot exist without authorship.
> Virtue depends on our ability to author for
> ourselves what we do in our daily lives....
> Virtue is the something new, the expanded

> good we bring to life. Being responsible
> equires that we acknowledge authorship of
> our actions and their consequences. Moral
> authority belongs to those who are willing to
> write their signature on their lives.[63]

What a powerful statement this is: parents, too, "author their children out of their own love, committing themselves to their growth into productive adulthood."[64] Hence, first we must author our own lives; then and only then can we begin to qualify as authors and moral authorities in our children's lives—and qualify we must.

It seems that it has become more and more difficult to master authority and authorship. We see these less and less frequently. Authority is easily confused with authoritarianism which has its base in power and allows for manipulation, coercion, and humiliation; none of these is healthy. Authoritarianism is about domination and power. Authoritarianism stunts growth: authority promotes it. Authority may be understood as energy expended not for its own sake but to be transformed through the process of its transmission into growth in others.[65] "Power is essentially amoral, sets its own standards, is indifferent to its agents, and is wedded to the instant out of which it flows. Authority is necessarily moral, reflective, and ordered to a future outcome that represents growth in itself as well as for the human beings affected by it."[66] Authority creates and maintains safety. People, whether husband and wife, employer and employee, or parent and child, need not be on guard against each other. Authority's job is to nurture the sound development of individuals as well as to look after the common good. Authority deals only in justice and fairness.

Emotionally healthy, prudent parents understand that they are in charge of the family; they do not give up their authorship of their children or family lifestyle. Although there will, of course, be conflict, their relationship with their children is not conflicted, confused nor harsh. It remains respectful, holds the children's best interest at heart, nurtures their potential and civility, and seeks their ultimate autonomy and freedom. Freedom does not imply nor include lack of structure or direction, both of which are important elements in child rearing. When authoring children, keeping them out of harm's way is necessary. As our mentor Ann Shorn warned us: children aren't careless by nature—they are carefree. Teaching them the lessons they each need is difficult and time-consuming work, yet this is the heart of authorship.

The concern is that if we, the parents, do not author our children, who will? The answer is others: school, television and video, other children, any aspect of our culture—anyone or anything who has influence. These other forces may have your child's best interest at heart, some of them may not. A few of these may be wise, many more will not be. This path is frightening. The bottom line: it takes responsible, respectful, prudent, self-controlled adults to author a child into the same type of adulthood. There are no shortcuts and easy ways. And in case you had any doubt, peers rarely author peers, certainly not as young children. There is a reason parents and children are from different generations and carry different statuses. Do not seek to be your child's friend. You are their parent!

Children must be allowed to *be* themselves in order that they may become themselves. In terms of interests, temperament, and childishness, children need to be children, not little adults. Authority recognizes this need. It does not make children live on adult schedules, going to dinner at 7:00 or 8:00 in the evening, missing naps, and staying out late. Neither does it encourage or allow children to reason before they are capable, nor to make decisions for which they are not ready, such as when one needs to go to bed, what foods are healthy, or where to go to school. Authority also understands that from a different perspective children must not be allowed to be themselves. That is to say, that we must not give in to childhood's natural proclivities. These areas include limiting inappropriate behaviors (hitting one's brother), supervising immature and dangerous behavior (eating junk food, not crossing streets holding hands), and imposing structure (bedtime is bedtime, you must play inside the fence, and no means no). Being able to distinguish where the line is between these is a key to carrying authority.

How do we author our children practically? First, we must know who we are and what we believe in and hold dear. Our values and principles must be clear. Second, we must be emotionally healthy, without issues and blinders and axes to grind. Third, we must not lack courage, for it takes courage to stay our own course. We must not be afraid to run against the grain. Fourth, we must know our job as parents and be unafraid to do it, whenever necessary and no matter how inconvenient. And fifth, we can use the activities and rituals of our daily life to teach our children what they need to know. Misbehavior often presents wonderful opportunities for lessons in character development. Good behavior, as well, offers opportunities to model or affirm character.

As stated earlier, the most overlooked and perhaps undervalued family ritual takes place at the family dinner table. It is worth saying again: when we gather together to share a meal and one another's companionship, we engage in something vital to our happiness as human beings. We strengthen the bonds which exist amongst us and use the time for a variety of purposes: playful affectionate interaction, answering questions stored up from the day, discussion of current world and political events, debriefing the pains and joys of the day, and finally, participation in the satisfaction that comes from nourishing our bodies together. We can, if we choose, also model caring and empathic listening. We can teach important manners and respectful meal time behavior. We can engage our families in problem solving and in planning the family's activities. We can teach older siblings that younger ones have thoughts and feelings about what is happening, and we can show younger ones that they can count on their family's support and help where it is needed.

Over the years I have heard of a variety of creative ways in which many families have preserved and enhanced this very special time together. Some families schedule regular candle-lit dinners or nag-free, manner-less meals. Others hold Sunday afternoon "high teas" with fancy china dishes and special treats. Still others focus on a particular family member one night per week, cooking her favorite meal and making that meal her special event. Some plan special topics for discussion: "All about boys" or "All about girls" or "What I like about school" and "What I hate about school." There is no denying that the more engaging we make the time spent together, the more we grow our connections. Do not feel, however, that every night at your house need feel like somebody's birthday. Sometimes—indeed most times—it is just a family sitting down to break bread together. You might want to consider this family rule about dinner time: if you are home when the family sits down to eat, then you come to the table and sit and keep the others company, whether you have eaten or not and whether you have other dinner plans. Food is not the issue: family time is. There needn't be anything special happening. It is just a gathering of family members together to be together at least once a day.

Spending time with our children, focused on them, in many other ways can also be very beneficial. Whether we are using great literature, fine art or music, the great outdoors, a sand box or a swing set, a mutual project or chore, or lying in a hammock communing with our children, the time is not simply well spent, it is well invested. We need to slow down here in North America; so do our children. Add the ritual of reading good books to your children and you continue to grow their understanding of what good character is. So many books offer our children the tools they need: "The best moral teaching inspires students by making them keenly aware that their own character is at stake."[67]

Indeed, for a parent to be able to author a child into her own mature adulthood, first that parent must have taken over authorship of himself. It is during the teen years that we see our children taking over their own identity-making. Clearly, by the time one is in his twenties, one must be authoring his own life. The nature of authority is that it helps people to become themselves. Authority's job is to make it possible for one to author one's own life: authority's goal is to put itself out of a job. What is involved? Kennedy and Charles state:

> The process includes the gradual refinement of the ability of growing persons to tell right from wrong on their own, for themselves. That means they can balance facts and circumstances against principles and tradition, distinguish the private right from the public good, and live in reasonable harmony with themselves and others.... Putting authority back into morals begins with formation of conscience. Rearing a child takes place on that energy curve of relationship between the parents and within the families to which they give life and growth.[68]

To speak with moral authority, one must speak with one's own voice. Moral authority urges others toward behavior for which they will have no regret—because it is the right behavior. It leads people to listen to their consciences, not to ignore or disobey them. When we stray from doing the right thing and when we fail to do what we know is right, our conscience, our good friend, guides us through guilt and healthy emotional homework: "I feel terrible; I feel awful. Of course, if I never do this wrong thing again, I will not have to feel this way. I am never doing this again." When we stay the course, when we do what is right, we feel right and experience no pain. There is no need for emotional homework. It is our job as parents not only to know what is right in the general world, but to seek out and discover what is right with parenting, the most important and most difficult of our jobs. It is this knowing that generates comfort for us in our positions as parents and informs our moral authority and authorship of our children. What could be better?

Taking Back Our Culture

Once upon a time, long, long ago it seems, our culture helped us to parent and both valued and backed us up as parents. No, this is not a fairy tale. It's true. It seems that nowadays we are on our own. To be good parents, we will have to rebel against the prevailing beliefs of our culture. It is sad, and it makes life more difficult, but this rebellion is necessary and inescapable. Let us look at some of the more obvious issues against which we need to rebel.

Society's Value for Children

Do we, as a society, really value children? The media and the government would have us believe so. There is a good deal of lip service and serious-faced acknowledgment of children's issues, but actions speak louder than words. If we genuinely cared about children, we would find ways to provide every child with easily and readily available health and dental care, and we would expect our social service agencies to be prevention focused and proactive. We would find ways to ensure that all children had access to good libraries, excellent athletic facilities, and opportunities to grow up well-nourished and safe from violence and harm. We would find ways to provide the best for our children, for everybody's children, simply because they are children. Let us not forget that they will ultimately take charge of this world. Make no mistake about it, the children of the under-privileged will share this country, this globe, with those whose accident of birth has made them privileged. All children have value and worth.

If we genuinely cared about children, and those who take care of them, would there not be a check-out line in the grocery store without candy, gum and trinkets to tempt these munchkins? If a store simply made one line without these temptations, wouldn't you be willing to wait patiently in that line with your children? Wouldn't you feel some gratitude and loyalty toward the store for understanding your position? (There seem to be a small but growing number of grocery stores which now have these! We need more.) Instead, our culture acts as though selling gum is more important than children and the job of parenting. I wonder why anyone who has ever sexually abused a child is ever considered safe amongst children. I wonder why we let repeat drunk driving offenders continue to drive. I marvel at parents who replace the car and pay the increased insurance for a son or daughter who has negligently wrecked a car and managed to live. Surely if we valued, really valued our children, we would protect them—whatever it takes.

Balance
Do you have balance in your life? Usually when I ask this question of a group of parents or teachers, I invariably hear laughter as the answer. What a sad state! What are we thinking? How can this be the culturally correct and acceptable answer, the assumption that balance is an impossible wish? Why is it alright not to have balance in our lives? Just how healthy can we be, emotionally as well as

physically, when we choose not to live balanced lives? What allows us to think for one moment that we can do the job of rearing children, universally acclaimed to be the hardest job, or any job for that matter, when we are continuously out of balance and stressed? What kind of life is this? When did balance cease to seem attainable?

We are a stressed nation: more importantly we are a nation who accepts stress. We work long hours. We work long days with no breaks. We fill any potential leisure time with purposeful activity. We do not know how to be still. We do not know how to relax. We do not know how to recreate—as in re-create. Why then are we surprised by road rage, parking lot rage and sports rage? This is a little too much. We need to slow things down, take breaks, recharge and find time to balance our lives.

Furthermore, we are passing this need for constant activity down to our children. There are three-year-olds with daytimers to keep track of their play dates, gymnastics class, drama class, etc. There is no time for play, for unstructured play not directed by an adult, for just being a child. Children, as they always have, need time simply to be children—joyful, free, and happy.

What about "down" time, that wonderful time in a child's or adult's life that is just spent contemplating the beauty of the world, the sweetness of a spring bird's song and the smell of wild violets? Our children need this time to find out who they are, what joys and perils the nature of the world around them offers, and to attempt to find their spiritual core. What is life without daydreams and playful wonderings of "what if"? Children need to role play being kings, queens, horses, chickens, mechanics, doctors, policemen, angels, eagles, beagles—you name it. In these playful imaginings come real learning and creative potential. In the sanctuary of play children build hidden reserves for the future. They learn how to have fun and how to be playful; in short, they learn about balance. Let's try to remember that when we take our children to piano or swimming lessons we should not be trying to make them better than other people's children, but better to and for themselves and their families.

Protecting Childhood

As Neil Postman explains in his book, *The Disappearance of Childhood,*[69] one of the finest developments or discoveries of the 20th Century was the concept of childhood. Previously, children were allowed a short period of infancy, followed by working and shouldering many adult responsibilities and burdens as early as age six or seven. Fortunately, over time we began to recognize that childhood was developmentally distinct, and with the industrial revolution we were, for the most part, able to afford to allow childhood to provide a reprieve, a time of moratorium, and a time mostly devoted to learning and development. It was a gift. It came from our understanding that children develop incrementally and are qualitatively different from adults. As a society we began to protect the time of childhood and in so doing we protected our children. One of the cardinal signs that there is a difference between children and adults is that children are not privy to the same information as adults. They did not need to know right away about the darker and heavier side of life, but this security is gradually slipping away. From the Internet to television, our children have access to everything and anything, from acts of violence to pornography to bomb-making.

To recreate and preserve this notion of childhood, we need to insulate our children from the effects of too much violence, sex, and consumerism and instead offer them activities which are more appropriate to their age and developmental understanding. Neil Postman describes the effect of rebelling against our culture and protecting childhood in this way:

> [T]here are parents who are committed to doing all of these things, who are in effect defying the directives of their culture. Such parents are not only helping their children to have a childhood but are, at the same time, creating a sort of intellectual elite. Certainly in the short run, the children who grow up in such homes will, as adults, be much favored by business, the professions, and the media themselves. What can we say of the long run? Only this: Those parents who resist the spirit of the age will contribute to what might be called the Monastery Effect, for they will help to keep alive a humane tradition. It is not conceivable that our culture will forget that it has children. But it is halfway toward forgetting that children need childhood. Those who insist on remembering shall perform a noble service for themselves and their children.[70]

I might add—a noble service for us all.

Healthy people must not be intimidated by a culture from which they feel estranged.
—Eugene Kennedy and Sara Charles, p. 38.

Resisting Peer Pressure

"Wrong is wrong even if everyone is doing it. Right is right even though no one does it."[71] —Wayne Dosick

Adolescent peer pressure is not the focus here; adult peer pressure is. Don't for a moment think it does not exist. We simply do not talk about it much. We must fight the "bad parent" pressure which tells us to enroll our children in any and all activities to keep them occupied and to keep other children from getting ahead, so that we can be perceived as good, involved parents. We must fight the competitive sport pressure that teaches our kids that winning at any cost is the goal. We forget that "sports don't develop character, they reveal it."[72] We must fight the financial pressure to buy more things, and the latest things, for our children so they can keep up. We must fight the every-one-is-doing-it pressure: "No one else has a bed time," and "Everyone's parents let their children watch PG-13 and R-rated movies before they are officially old enough." Previously, in Chapter Six, we discussed the media. Here I would like to add that limiting "screen" access in both quantity and quality is an act of rebellion—one of our most important. Indeed, preserving our children, preserving our own family values is an almost constant running battle and requires frequent discussion and running commentary with our children about the actions of others and governments surrounding us. It means we must challenge the values of our culture.

Helplessness and Weakness
"Absolute powerlessness corrupts absolutely."[73] —Steven Carr Reuben

How often do we excuse our behavior and our failings with defenses concerning gender, age or circumstances: "Girls are like that," "Boys will be boys," "You can't get through to teens"? These are all feeble attempts to explain away our ineptness, our laziness, and our cowardice. These excuses allow us to be socially acceptable victims, to continue with our learned helplessness. We are not victims, and children need and deserve better. Our children need parents who will not succumb to cheap excuses for doing the wrong thing, but who will encourage them to act upon their best impulses and with good, solid character.

"I Did My Best"

I have yet to meet a natural parent. No one does the job of parenting easily. It is an overwhelming responsibility for which most of us have not been prepared or perhaps have been prepared poorly. Despite our recognition of the need for education, training and practice in any other field, we think two hours of lecture in parenting and one or two books will suffice. Or, we think because having our children is instinctive, we can rely solely on inborn skills which we apparently come by naturally. I don't think so. We need instead to conscientiously reflect on, establish, and internalize who we wish to be as parents and what character traits we wish our children to learn. We need to actively seek out understanding and then skills. We need to see and remember that the "experts" in this field disagree, as they do in every field. Furthermore, some of them are wrong for us, our families and our society. Who decides? You do. But not without careful thought, soul-searching, and courage. Seeking age-old wisdom and truth can help guide us. Holding fast to principles like the Law of the Harvest and the Golden Rule will not fail us, either as codes of conduct or as tools for teaching and growing.

It is not enough to say—and try to believe—that we did our best when we really haven't. When we put so little time, energy and reflection into this vital commitment, how can we say that it was our best? We committed ourselves by bringing these children into our lives. That is inescapable. What many of us don't realize is how much we owe them.

Decide who you are. Decide who your family is and what its core values are and will be. Decide what is acceptable and what must be addressed and changed. Each and every day actively teach lessons with love, discipline, stories, conversation, books, hugs—whatever you can find and whatever it takes. You hold the future in your hands. You hold your children in your hands—for a time. You also hold your integrity and character in your hands.

> We who lived in concentrations camps can remember the men who walked through the huts comforting others, giving away their last piece of bread. They may have been few in number, but they offer sufficient proof that everything can be taken away from a man but one thing: the last of the human freedoms—to choose one's attitude in any given set of circumstances, to choose one's own way.
> —Victor Frankl

Chapter Checkpoints

✔ Part of our job as parents is to help author our children. This must be done only with their best interests at heart.

✔ It takes moral courage not to be intimidated by our culture. All too often our culture is unhelpful and leads us down the wrong path.

✔ Children must be allowed to be children.

✔ Children must be grown into adults.

✔ If we, the parents, do not author good strong character, who will? We must schedule, find and take the time to do this.

✔ Good authorship teaches a child to be the author of his own life.

✔ We must rebel against our own culture when we disaagree with its precepts, expectations or values.

✔ We must put into action our strong value for children. We will need to continue to protect childhood.

✔ Balance in our own lives is an essential ingredient to healthy living, let alone healthy parenting.

✔ In parenting, no one gives you permission. You own all of your choices and all of your behavior.

✔ Think long and hard before pronouncing, "I did my best." Then, do your best.

1. Neil Postman, *Building a Bridge to the Eighteenth Century: How the Past Can Improve Our Future* (New York: Alfred A. Knopf, 1999), 129.

2. T. Berry Brazelton, "Values that Make a Strong Family," *Family Circle.* Retrieved from http://www.parents.com/cgi-bin/WebObjects/Parents/PM.woa/0619100000308410000.../gruner

3. Dalai Lama and H. C. Cutler, *The Art of Happiness* (New York: Riverhead Press, 1998).

4. Dalai Lama and Cutler.

5. The original quote is, "No one can make you feel inferior without your permission."

6. J. B. Miller and I. P. Stiver, *The Healing Connection* (Boston, MA: Beacon Press, 1997).

7. J. B. Miller and I. P. Stiver.

8. J. B. Miller and I. P. Stiver.

9. The American Heritage® Dictionary of the English Language, Third Edition copyright © 1992 by Houghton Mifflin Company. Electronic version licensed from InfoSoft International, Inc. All rights reserved.

10. Dalai Lama and H. C. Cutler, 51.

11. The American Heritage® Dictionary of the English Language, Third Edition copyright © 1992 by Houghton Mifflin Company. Electronic version licensed from InfoSoft International, Inc. All rights reserved.

12.   Margaret Anderson, *Raising a Family is a Pleasure* (n.d., n.p., out of print). I am indebted to Mike Anderson for sharing this helpful and wise text with me.

13.   Madelyn Swift, *Discipline for Life: Getting it Right with Children* (Fort Worth, TX: Childright, 1999).

14.   Steve Testrake, submission to *Weekend Encounter.* Retrieved from weekend-encounter-request @gospelcom.net(e-mail)

15.   Fredelle Maynard, "Perspectives," *Homemaker's Magazine,* May 1989, 118.

16.   Jean Illsley Clarke and Connie Dawson, *Growing Up Again: Parenting Ourselves, Parenting Our Children* (New York: HarperCollins, 1989).

17.   Jean Illsley Clarke, *Connections: The Threads That Strengthen Families* (Center City, MN: Hazelden, 1999).

18.   Ervin Staub, "Aggression and Self-esteem," *Monitor on Psychology,* Volume 30, Number 1, January, 1999. I am indebted to this article for this paragraph's information.

19.   Lilian G. Katz, "Self-Esteem and Narcissism: Implications for Practice," *ERIC Clearinghouse on Elementary and Early Childhood Education.* Retrieved from http://www.ericeece.org/pubs/ digests/1993/lk-sel93.html

20.   Madelyn Swift.

21. Mary Pipher, *The Shelter of Each Other: Rebuilding Our Families* (New York: G. P. Putnam's Sons, 1996).

22. Madelyn Swift.

23. Anonymous story from the Internet.

24. Bob Chase, "NEA President at the Fourth Annual Character Counts! Coalition Meeting," Washington DC, April 11, 1997. Retrieved from http://www.nea.org/nr/sp971104.html

25. Anonymous story from the Internet.

26. S. C. Reuben, *Children of Character: A Parent's Guide* (Santa Monica, CA: Canter & Associates, Inc., 1997), 130.

27. S. C. Reuben.

28. A good children's book store or department often has a resident expert who can lead you to great stories and/or books. Don't just buy any children's book, buy children's literature. *The Moral Compass: Stories for a Life's Journey* edited by William J. Bennett is a wonderful starting point. As well, Jim Trelease's *The Read-Aloud Handbook* offers and describes many children's books.

29. B. S. Bowden and J. M. Zeisz, "Family Meals May Prevent Teen Problems," *APA Monitor,* October 1997, 28(10): 8.

30. David Walsh, *Selling Out America's Children: How America Puts Profits Before Values and What Parents Can Do.* A summary for Parent News by Peggy Patten. Retrieved from http://www.npin.org/news1998/pnew1198/int1198.html

31.   David Walsh.

32.   James McNeal and Chyon-Hwa Yeh, "Born to Shop,"
       American Demographics, June 1993: 34-39.

33.   James McNeal, "Mapping the Three Kids' Markets,"
       American Demographics, April 1998: 37-41.

34.   Brian Swimme, *The Hidden Heart of the Cosmos*
       (Marknoll, NY: Orbis Books, 1996).

35.   M. F. Jacobson and L. A. Mazur, *Marketing Madness*
       (Boulder: Westview Press, 1995), 22.

36.   Brian Swimme.

37.   J. Hadley, "Credit Cards Get Students in a Hole,
       Fast," *Seattle Post Intelligencer,* May 11, 1998.
       Retrieved from http://www.bea.doc.gov/bea/
       glance.html

38.   Mary Pipher.

39.   David Walsh.

40.   "Tips for Parenting in a Commercial Culture."
       Retrieved from newdream@newdream.org

41.   S. C. Reuben, 53.

42.   S. C. Reuben, 53.

43.   S. C. Reuben.

44.   W. J. Bennett, *The Book of Virtues: A Treasury of
       Great Moral Stories* (New York: Simon & Schuster,
       1993).

45. W. J. Bennett, *The Moral Compass* (New York: Simon & Schuster, 1995).

46. E. Berger, *Raising Children with Character: Parents, Trust, and the Development of Personal Integrity* (Northvale, NJ: Jason Aronson Inc., 1999).

47. David Walsh.

48. S. C. Reuben, 130.

49. Tips indicated with * are excerpted from Margaret Anderson's book, *Raising a Family is a Pleasure.*

50. Margaret Anderson.

51. Margaret Anderson.

52. *Webster's Seventh New Collegiate Dictionary* (Springfield, MA: G. & C. Merriam Company, 1967).

53. Sharon Begley, "The Roots of Evil," *Newsweek,* 21 May 2001.

54. Sharon Begley.

55. Sharon Begley.

56. Sharon Begley.

57. Sharon Begley.

58. Sharon Begley.

59. Nel Jackson, "Lead by Example - Character is Catching." Retrieved from http://www.character. org/action/newslet.cgi?winter_1998:lead Quotation by Ken Barun.

60.   E. Kennedy & S. C. Charles, *Authority* (New York: The Free Press, 1997), 4.

61.   E. Kennedy & S. C. Charles, 2.

62.   E. Kennedy & S. C. Charles, 2.

63.   E. Kennedy & S. C. Charles, 4.

64.   E. Kennedy & S. C. Charles.

65.   E. Kennedy & S. C. Charles, 4.

66.   E. Kennedy & S. C. Charles, 35.

67.   Christina Hoff Sommers, "Teaching the Virtues," *Chicago Tribune Magazine*, 15 November 1992: 18.

68.   E. Kennedy & S. C. Charles.

69.   Neil Postman, *The Disappearance of Childhood* (New York: Vintage Books, 1994).

70.   Neil Postman, *Building a Bridge to the Eighteenth Century: How the Past Can Improve Our Future* (New York: Alfred A. Knopf, 1999), 129-130.

71.   Wayne Dosick, *Golden Rules: The Ten Ethical Values Parents Need to Teach Their Children* (New York: HarperCollins Publisher, 1995), 48.

72.   Darrell J. Burnett, "Teaching Youngsters How to be Good Sports (Part 1 of 6)." Retrieved from http://www.youth-sports.com/getpage.cfm?file=/topics/feb98-08.html&userid=10335202 Quotation by Heywood Hale Broun.

73.   S. C. Reuben, 163.

Anderson, M. (n.d., n.p., out of print). *Raising a Family is a Pleasure.* Self-published.

Begley, S. (2001, May 21). The Roots of Evil. *Newsweek.*

Berger, E. (1999). *Raising Children with Character: Parents, Trust, and the Development of Personal Integrity.* Northvale, NJ: Jason Aronson Inc.

Bennett, W. J., editor. (1995). *The Moral Compass: Stories for a Life's Journey.* New York: Simon & Schuster.

Bennett, W. J. (1993). *The Book of Virtues: A Treasury of Great Moral Stories.* New York: Simon & Schuster.

Bowden, B. S. and J. M. Zeisz. (1997, October). Family Meals May Prevent Teen Problems. *APA Monitor,* 28(10)8.

Brazelton, T. B. (1997, July). Values that Make a Strong Family. *Family Circle.* Retrieved from http://www.parents.com/cgi-bin/WebObjects/Parents/PM.woa/0619100000308410000.../gruner

Burnett, D. J. (1998, February). Teaching Youngsters How to be Good Sports. Retrieved from http://www.youth-sports.com/getpage.cfm?file=/topics/feb98-08.html&userid=10335202

Clarke, J. I. (1999). *Connections: The Threads That Strengthen Families.* Center City, MN: Hazelden.

Clarke, J. I. and C. Dawson. (1989). *Growing Up Again: Parenting Ourselves, Parenting Our Children.* New York: HarperCollins.

Dalai Lama and H. C. Cutler. (1998). *The Art of Happiness.* New York: Riverside Press.

Dosick, W. (1995). *Golden Rules: The Ten Ethical Values Parents Need to Teach Their Children.* New York: HarperCollins Publisher.

Hadley, J. (1998, May). Credit Cards Get Students in a Hole, Fast. *Seattle Post Intelligencer.* Retrieved from http://www.bea.doc.gov.bea.glance.html

Jackson, N. (1998, winter). Lead by Example - Character is Catching. Retrieved from http://www.character. org/action/newslet.cgi?winter_1998:lead

Katz, L. (1993). Self-Esteem and Narcissism: Implications for Practice. *ERIC Clearinghouse on Elementary and Early Childhood Education.* Retrieved from http://www.ericeece.org/pubs/digests/1993/lk-sel93.html

Kennedy, E. and S. C. Charles. (1997). *Authority: The Most Misunderstood Idea in America.* New York: The Free Press.

Maynard, F. (1989, May). Perspectives. *Homemaker's Magazine.*

McNeal, J. (1998, April). Mapping the Three Kids' Markets. *American Demographics.*

Miller, J. B. and I. P. Stiver. (1997). *The Healing Connection.* Boston, MA: Beacon Press.

Pipher, M. (1996). *The Shelter of Each Other: Rebuilding Our Families.* New York: G. P. Putnam's Sons.

Postman, N. (1999). *Building a Bridge to the Eighteenth Century: How the Past Can Improve Our Future.* New York: Alfred A. Knopf.

Postman, N. (1994). *The Disappearance of Childhood.* New York: Vintage Press.

Reuben, S. C. (1997). *Children of Character: A Parent's Guide.* Santa Monica, CA: Canter & Associates, Inc.

Staub, E. (1999, January). Aggression and Self-esteem. *Monitor on Psychology,* 30 (1).

Sommers, C. H. (1992, November 15). Teaching the Virtues. *Chicago Tribune Magazine.*

Swift, M. (1999). *Discipline for Life: Getting it Right with Children.* Fort Worth, TX: Childright.

Swimme, B. (1996). *The Hidden Heart of the Cosmos.* Marknoll, NY: Orbis Books.

Walsh, D. (1998). *Selling Out America's Children: How America Puts Profits Before Values and What Parents Can Do.* A summary for Parent News by Peggy Patten. Retrieved from http://npin.org.news1998/pnew1198/int1198.html